Contemplating Illness

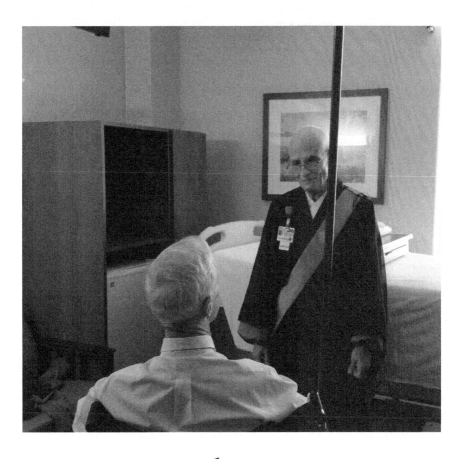

by
Ryusho Jeffus

The wonderful chaplains I worked with at CMC-Mercy Hospital in Charlotte, North Carolins. Left to right: Chaplain Terri Bolotin, Chaplain Ryusho Jeffus, Chaplain Eric Guthrie. This photo was taken in the chapel of Mercy Hospital.

Contemplating Illness

By Ryusho Jeffus
Copyright 2019

Myosho-ji, Wonderful Voice Buddhist Temple
611 Vine St.
Syracuse, NY 13203

ISBN-13: 9781097885008
Imprint: Independently Published

Dedication

I would like to dedicate this book to the following:

First to all the young boys who I sat with and cared for who died way too young from AIDS without them I may never have gone on to do this work I do. I dedicate my efforts to the lessons they taught me and the gifts they gave to me.

I would like to thank the many people who later helped me refine my knowledge and fashion into something useful and with a semblance of wisdom. My shortcomings are not their fault.

The following names are in no particular known order though probanbly on some deep subconcions level there is a reason. Terri Bolotin, Eric Gutherie, Rebekah Ramsey, Angela Janssen-Keenan, Angela Clarke, David Carl, David Jackson, Moses Taiwo, Barbara Bullock, Malu Fairley, Beth Jackson-Jordan, Elizabeth Morse, as well as all the nurses, administration, environmental services people I met and worked alongside during my time working for Carolinas Healthcare System, now Atrium. I would also like to offer a special appreciation to Miss Dot who passed away several years ago. She servied the meals and looked out for all the residents both medical and chaplain and made sure we were amply nourished. I owuld also like to thank Alicia Thomas aka "Pinky" a special food services worker at Mercy Hospital who always had a smile and encouraging word and never failed to call me Father even though I am not that kind of religion, lol. Also my gratitude goes to Miss B who never listened when I said my portion of food was sufficient and always insisted I needed more on my plate.

I have tried to remember names of everyone though I am sure I have failed to remember all. For those who have been left out please know it was not intentional and I will happily make the correction in future printings.

Contents

1

Introduction

For the majority of my life I have in one way or another engaged in caring for people suffering from various diseases and illnesses. First, taking care of boys dying from AIDS. Then as a Board Certified Chaplain, BCC and working as a staff chaplain in a major hospital in Charlotte, NC.

As I read through Paul L. Swanson's translation of T'ien-T'ai Chih-I's Mo-Ho Chih-Kuan: Clear Serenity, Quiet Insight I began mulling over, sitting with, ruminating, meditating on the section "Contemplating the Objects of Disease." Every living being endures in some form or another disease and suffering. Since so much of my life's work has been in this realm, I feel strongly compelled to offer my insights from studying this section in the hopes that it may be of benefit to others.

In the Lotus Sutra, Chapter XV, "The Appearance of Bodhisattvas from Underground," we have the story of the emergence of unprecedented Bodhisattvas who emerge from beneath the earth in response to the Buddha's questioning who would spread the Dharma of the Lotus Sutra in the later age of degeneration after his death. These great bodhisattvas are lead by four bodhisattvas. As the Four Leader Bodhisattvas approached the Buddha they said "World-Honored One, are you peaceful? Are you in good health?"[1] This is

1   Translated by Senchu Murano, The Lotus Sutra: The Sutra of the Lotus Flower of the Wonderful Dharma, 2012, Nichiren Shu, page 236

a variation on a standard greeting exchanged between Buddhas. It is also variously translated "May you have little disease and little suffering."[2]

I have pointed out in various other writings how remarkable even the act of making an enquiry into the wellbeing of the Buddha is in the Lotus Sutra. Throughout the Lotus Sutra the interactions between the Buddha and various people in the congregation were all requests made to the Buddha to predict that person's future enlightenment. It was only these Bodhisattvas who represent us who asked how the Buddha was doing.

I've frequently thought of most of the Lotus Sutra as a Mardi Gras parade in New Orleans. I was a child growing in New Orleans and, as everyone who has been there during Mardi Gras knows, the chants at all the parades are "Throw me something mister" – Throw me some cheap beads, throw me some candy, throw me a doubloon, throw me a prediction of my enlightenment, throw me a tale of my future good deeds. Well, I can always manage to be a bit irreverent.

One thing we learn from this is that even Buddhas have disease, they are not immune to the four sufferings of birth, sickness, decay, and death. Every being, every human being will have disease. Now we are not speaking only of diagnosable diseases or only those things that may bring us to the doctor's office or hospital.

One of my supervisors in my training as a chaplain frequently would say disease is diss ease – to not be at ease. There is quite some wisdom loaded in this turn of the phrase and that's one of the things I hope to share with you from a Buddhist perspective and specifically from a Lotus Sutra based view from Chih-i.

---

2   Translated by Paul L. Swanson, T'ien-T'ai Chih-I's Mo-Ho Chih-Kuan: Clear Serenity, Quiet Insight Vol 3, Honolulu, University of Hawai'i Press, 2018, page 1322

2

Two Meanings

Disease is a fact of existence. Chih-i considered disease to be of two types: real and tentative. We must not be misled by the use of tentative, however, as being something that only is of short duration or that will simply go away. A tentative disease is a disease of instruction. An example would be the illness of Vimalakirti, the famous Mahayana lay Buddhist practitioner.

In the story of Vimalakirti he becomes very ill, bedridden in fact. The Buddha, upon hearing of Vimalakirti's illness, sends his senior disciples one after another to inquire after Vimalakirti's health and to offer assistance. One by one, these famous senior disciples are humbled by Vimalakirti. That is, he causes them to humble themselves as he demonstrates various truths of Buddhism to these senior and quite accomplished followers of the Buddha. It gets to the point that some disciples really don't want to go and be embarrassed by this person who was only a lay practitioner.

Vimalakirti took on the aspect of disease for the purpose of teaching. This is what is meant by tentative disease. We can set this concept of tentative disease aside. Our contemplation here is on actual diseases.

Generally, you go through life and you feel fine. You see yourself in good health. Occasionally, you might have a cold or flu or an upset stomach. Perhaps you take some over-the-counter remedy and the symptoms go away. No big deal. And then one day you're feeling fine, and you go to the doctor and the doctor tells you something is going on inside you that you were unaware of happening.

This happens very often. I've witnessed it in my hospital work and I've experienced it personally. About a year ago, while I was living in North Carolina, I began losing weight and I brought it to the attention of my various doctors at the Veterans Administration hospital where I receive health care. In spite of my concerns the doctor dismissed my concerns. When I moved to Syracuse my new doctor got curious about it. She ordered a series of X-rays and CAT scans. When all the various tests had been finished an appointment was scheduled for me to go over the results.

To keep this story short, let me say it's not a good thing when your doctor draws a picture of a pretty flower and says that's the shape of a tumor the tests found in your lung. It exhibits the growth pattern of cancer and not a good kind.

Every three months I've gone in for follow-up CAT scans and pulmonary checks. The good news is there has been no growth of the tumor and the VA is going to switch to a two-year cycle, assuming the tumor is benign. The other news, which is not bad, is that this assessment is uncertain.

When people have asked me about the tumor, I've compared it to an unwelcome house guest. You don't want the them in your house yet they won't leave. So, you have this truce: You will feed them and house them, and they agree to keep quiet, behave themselves and stay in their room. Well, that's been my arrangement.

Sometimes we may have a disease and be acutely aware of the illness and at other times completely unaware.

The truth, which we like to forget or ignore, is that we will suffer disease. Perhaps this is because we are further and further removed from disease. Disease and illness happen someplace else – in a doctor's office, in a hospital, at a neighbor's, or someplace viewed on TV. In ages not so long ago, we were much more intimate with disease. You knew when your neighbor had an illness. You needed to know this, especially if it was contagious. You knew when the local doctor was making a house call. Now people go to the doctor and this is treated as a private matter. Disease is less communal.

When we are experiencing an absence of disease, it would be healthier for us to realize that these times are temporary, and truly gifts not to be taken for granted. From a Buddhist perspective, disease is a condition of life. The absence of disease is temporary at best. In fact, an absence really means you have "less" disease to the point of being unaware. The constant condition of life tends towards disease.

3

Balance, Harmony, and Whack

To have physical form is to have disease. Why, you might ask? Besides the obvious answer that a physical body is subject to decay and change, it is because of the natural imbalance of our physical life. Our bodies are comprised of the four elements of earth, water, air, and fire. That may sound a tad bit archaic or even suspiciously superstitious and certainly not the language of modern medicine. Remember, though, that we are not talking about the modern practice of medicine, diagnosing specific illnesses, prescribing complex and expensive medicines.

Yet, even modern medicine still fundamentally is trying to overcome the imbalance of the four elements in our bodies, trying to overcome the causes of our illnesses. Too much blood pressure is water out of balance. Chronic Obstructive Pulmonary Disease, COPD, is a function of earth and air. Arthritis a function of earth. Fever is a function of fire, which must be maintained within a certain range for our bodies to be healthy.

To begin with, these four elements are in opposition to each other even outside our bodies. Fire and water and earth and wind are naturally opposites and are in a constant struggle. Chih-i compares the struggle between the four elements to four neighboring countries who are constantly at war with each other. As long as the strength of each country is equal, then there is a peace, or rather a cessation of hostilities. The moment one country has an advantage, then it will attack the weaker and war resumes.

Whether you think of earth, wind, fire and water isn't critical as long as you keep in mind that any treatment for disease is an attempt to restore your body to a harmonious state. We could say that clogged arteries are a condition of earth and water warring with each other, though, again, you don't need to use those terms. Whether you have a procedure to clear out the arteries or take a medication, the intent is to remove the blockage so your blood flows freely.

Dietary guidelines are an attempt to offer suggestions for the better maintenance of the harmony of the four elements in your body. Or, in modern terms, they are suggested so that your body's good health is maintained.

When we become ill our first thought isn't, "What's out of balance?" Most times it is "What can I take to make the pain or discomfort or condition go away?" Whether your doctor uses terms reflecting harmony or four elements, your doctor is indeed seeking to find out what is out of whack. High blood pressure, arthritis, swollen glands, sore throat, toothache and so on through the miles-long list of possible ailments are all terms to more precisely define "out of harmony" or "out of whack."

Chih-i refers to the four elements as snakes. An explanation for the metaphor of four snakes can be found in the Suvarnaprabhasa Sutra, which offers a parable of a man who, fleeing from the two bewildering forms of life and death, spies a rope (life) and climbs down into the well of impermanence. In this well are two mice who night and day gnaw on the rope. The platted rattan rope is of four sides and on each of the sides is a snake which is trying to poison our fleeing man. These four snakes are the four elements of the man's physical nature. As if this were not bad enough, below him are three fire-breathing dragons who are not only trying to burn him to a crisp they are also trying to grab him in their talons. Above, he sees two elephants, representing darkness and light, have come to the mouth of the well.[1] The poor wretched man is in complete despair when suddenly a bee flies by and drops honey into the man's mouth. The honey represents the five desires. The man eats the honey and completely forgets his peril.

As I read this I thought of the Lotus Sutra and the children playing in the burning house. They are so engrossed in playing that they are oblivious to the fire that is raging around them. And there, too, the fire is not the only hazard. There are numerous beasts and poisonous animals infesting the house. It almost sounds like they were playing video games and had been sucked into the vortex of the game experience.

Another reference to snakes being the four elements can be found in the Mahaparinirvana Sutra which offers an exercise for us to consider.

Exercise: "...contemplate the body as like a box [containing] earth, water, fire, and wind like four poisonous snakes. They see poison, touch poison, feel poison, gnaw on poison. All sentient beings encounter these four poisons, and mourn their life. The four elements of sentient beings are also like this."[2]

This skin bag of bones is fundamentally suffering due to its existence. This can be a depressing thought. For some it may be frightening. We tend to want our lives to be more than this, to mean more than this, to be more important than this. And that is our suffering. Like our friend in the well we have tasted the honey and all too easily forget our peril. In our rush to level up in the video game of life we forget our mortality and our impermanence. We seek a harmony of the four elements that can only be temporary at best no matter how much we desire it to last forever.

What keeps this from being depressing, at least for me, is the knowledge that the impermanence is a promise and a guarantee. It is

---

1   ibid 1322
2   ibid 1322

the thing to count on. Embracing impermanence can be liberating in that there is no surprise. Keeping impermanence foremost in mind motivates me not to forget the value of even a single moment of life and the infinite possibilities to fill each moment with value.

Our lives, this box containing the snakes of four elements, is frequently taken for granted. We've all heard stories of people who went into a doctor's office for an annual exam only to learn they have just months to live. When I worked as a chaplain I met people who were admitted for a condition they thought would be quickly cured only to find they had days to live, or whose lingering headache was a brain hemorrhage and death followed in hours.

People rarely factor in their mortality as they navigate their lives daily or hourly, yet death is perhaps only a breath away.

Exercise: Do this lightly! During your next meditation, or even in this moment, pay attention to your breath. As you breathe out, consider that this breath out is the only thing guaranteed to us. When we die that final breath out will be expelled from our lungs and never be replaced. Then, as you breathe in, feel the joy of life enter your lungs. The breath in is not guaranteed to any of us. We are only a breath away from our mortality. Do this lightly!

4

Resting in Forbearance

Diseases to be contemplated here include a wide range of karmic diseases, or diseases that are ours because we have a physical body. We are in this case speaking of karma in a general and broad sense and not to any specific karmic disease.

Besides the suffering of the disease there is the additional negative impact on one's faith and practice. I know from experiences that a simple cold or sinus infection can impact my daily practice. When your body aches, or you feel weak or nauseated, it is challenging even to sit down to change the water or offer tea, or light candles and incense, and then simply chant Odaimoku three times. I have, I admit, lain in bed and skipped the ritual for a day.

We think of our Buddhist practice as a journey. We commonly speak of walking the path of our Buddhist practice, or the path of faith. We don't, however, say the same things about illness or disease and yet those, too, are a journey, perhaps through pain, or through inconvenience, or even to death. Chih-i brings up the comparison of managing illness to traveling.

If you've ever taken a long trip, and especially a very long trip away from home, you are probably aware that it can be challenging to maintain a steady practice. There may be some days when you don't practice at all other than chanting some Odaimoku silently to yourself. Don't worry about this. You won't be punished. There is no punishment for not practicing in Buddhism. There is simply the absence of those valuable causes that we make when we practice.

With a continual strong regular practice, we accumulate a wealth of good fortune. That is one reason why the Buddha frequently mentions that the benefits of our Buddhist faith are immeasurable. How is it possible to measure unlimited? It's simply unlimited. With the accumulated good fortune, we can afford to miss some practice and still have a strong faith. Of course, it isn't possible to coast for very long because immeasurable, as unlimited as it may be, has limits. Crazy huh?

So, you're traveling and you miss some days, no worries. Simply resume again when you can. Don't add stress to your already stressful situation. However, you know deep inside whether you are being lazy and if so that of course should sound alarm bells, even klaxons warning: DANGER! DANGER! DANGER!

Traveling is disruptive, even if it is fun. Our regular schedule is not so regular at times, our rhythm is not so rhythmical. And sometimes it is hard to sort out what time it really is, especially with international travel.

With illness it may not seem quite the same and yet it is. The pain or discomfort has a way of blending all days into one day, or parts of a day into one long blur. I met a patient in dialysis once who told me he had adjusted to the reality of his once-every-two-days dialysis treatment by going to a 48-hour day.

For those not familiar with dialysis, you go in one day completely drained of energy and wiped out when you finish your treatment. For roughly six to eight hours you are close to non-functional. Then for the next 40 or so hours (minus your eight hours of normal sleep) you are full of energy. On a 24-hour day that means that every other day you have no energy or capacity to do anything.

For this patient, focusing on a 48-hour day was a mental practice that allowed him to tolerate dialysis. It is like a long night with a very long day. So, he adapted, and learned to live with his disease.

The journey of illness is part of managing its impact on our lives.

A trait this dialysis patient manifested is forbearance. Chih-i talks about the practice of forbearance being critical in our contemplation of disease. How we tolerate the intolerable, how we endure the unbearable, how we practice self-control when everything seems to be out of our control. Yet these are exactly the conditions of our life in every moment, even when we don't think we are sick or have a disease.

Some people live life in a leisurely way, taking things for granted, assuming there is all the time in the world to accomplish things, or that this smooth situation will continue indefinitely. This is a neon-lit doorway inviting in Mara, the devil who seeks to block or hinder our practice. So too is resignation and hopelessness in the face of difficulty, disease, or illness. Mara sees these and knows he only needs to bring half his army because you are already defeated.

Some people use their good times to great advantage, others slack off. Some people use adversity to great advantage, while others give up. Simply having a disease or an illness does not determine what our response will be, our nature and tendency do. This is our karma, not the disease or the good fortune. It is what we do with either condition.

5

Comforting the Ill

At this point I'd like to make a little detour away from Chih-i and return to Vimalakirti. I mentioned earlier that the illnesses we are talking about do not cover those taken on for the purpose of instruction, such as the illness of Vimalakirti. Yet in the Vimalakirti Sutra we can learn important lessons, such as found in the exchange between Manjushri and Vimalakirti on how to encourage a bodhisattva who has illness.

Before we take up Vimalakirti and the wisdom found in the sutra I'd like offer some examples of situations for your consideration. Working as a chaplain, I had many opportunities to witness not only illness but hopelessness, and not only the hopelessness of the sick patient but the hopelessness of those who wished to encourage or support the patient. Many people simply did not know how to be supportive, and worried about making things worse for the patient.

It is a challenge to be supportive and yet remain honest, to offer encouragement without offering false hope, to be honest about an illness and its effects without either making them worse or discounting them.

One classic example is the compulsion to get a family member to eat when they are dying. There is an almost universal belief that if a person just eats somehow that will be the key to their recovery. While that can certainly be the case, it is not always.

Take dying for example. When a person is dying, the body knows it doesn't need food, which only interferes with the process. This is difficult for family members to accept. While doctors can be reasonably certain about this, there remains some uncertainty. This is where the family and those close to the patient can offer the medical staff some insight, but it is hard to do. It requires those supporting the patient to set aside fears and consider what may be happening and what are certain natural behaviors of the patient.

All too often the dread of losing the patient clouds the support person's ability to see things realistically. This is where it is critical to listen to what the medical personal are saying and then look at the patient with the possibility that the medical diagnosis is correct while not completely abandoning hope for a different outcome. One can remain encouraging while being honest, remain hopeful without dismissing the real possibility of loss.

In many ways it is very beneficial for the patient because they know they can express their fears openly, and they will be heard and honored. It's tough for a patient who inwardly knows they are dying and trying to work through that process while everyone around them is saying no, or don't talk like that, or other such dismissive attitudes.

It is a complicated process, an intricate dance, if you will, between those supporting the patient and the patient, between honesty and grief and hope and reality. In my experience the closer people come to being honest – about their fears and their grief as well as their hope – the deeper the final conversations can be. There are many excellent books written by Buddhists and non-Buddhists that are worth reading before the need arises. They offer insight, ideas, examples and wisdom. It really isn't possible for one book or one person to have all the answers so my offering here is merely one person's view based on my experiences.

When the body is in the dying process it is actively engaging in eliminating all unnecessary body functions. Digesting food takes a lot of energy, and the food being consumed isn't really offering its full nutritional value because the body isn't fully processing it in the way it would if it were healthy. The body tries to get rid of it and so it is an energy drain without the benefit of gain. Also, as the body is shutting down it naturally produces pain relieving 'medications'. Consuming food interferes with this process.

The body can go a long time without food, a week or more. It can't go quite as long without water. The care facility will be adequately monitoring this or, if at home, small sips of water might be advisable but consult with a qualified provider and don't rely on my advice alone. I am merely offering an overview of the mechanics of the body dying so as to help caregivers understand what's going on.

The body could produce powerful pain-relieving compounds and will do so even in the dying process. What hospice or hospitals can do is monitor the situation and supplement the natural process to administer small doses of more potent pain meds if necessary to keep the patient comfortable.

Here's something I found most people don't realize about pain medications unless they have been on the receiving end: Morphine, a common pain medication given in hospitals, causes constipation. You probably know this is very uncomfortable. Now if the patient is being forced or cajoled into eating when the body is shutting down, more pain meds are needed because the body's natural process has been interrupted. More pain meds mean more constipation. Now laxatives need to be given to counteract the constipation which in turn causes diarrhea which is uncomfortable and increases the need for anal maintenance, which can hurt tender skin.

A whole cascade of measures and countermeasures need to be taken to keep feeding a body that is trying not to consume food in order for it to do its thing naturally. What was intended to be supportive, encouraging the patient to eat, now becomes a hindrance and harmful.

This is one of many things about the dying process and about illness that we as a society are ill-prepared for.

It's not just family and friends who don't know how to interact with the patient. I've witnessed many doctors who, while good at the practice and delivery of medicine are woefully inadequate in finding the balance between honesty and compassion. I'll say this from witnessing many doctor-patient interactions: Most doctors don't know how to deliver bad news. Part of this comes from the sense of failure on the part of the doctor unable to cure a disease or prevent death.

In my time working in a cardiac ICU, I did see more and more younger physicians who were quite willing to be honest and had also mastered the art of doing so while being genuinely compassionate. They were quite skilled at speaking not just from a professional position but also from a humane voice. I benefited greatly during my time there from the many invitations by physicians to be present when the "bad news" had to be delivered and I'll say they did commendable jobs in the face of extremely emotional interactions.

Now let's turn to Vimalakirti. In the chapter Inquiring About Illness, Vimalakirti offers several guides in how to comfort and instruct another bodhisattva who is ill. As I thought about these I considered that for most of them there is a universal truth, although the words need to be changed for the individual and circumstances. I do believe that overall, they are more helpful than such cliché expressions of non-Buddhist faiths such as, it's God's plan, or God needs another angel in heaven. Even some Buddhist denominations suggest that if you chant or pray enough you can overcome this. To that I say, "How much chanting do you have to do to prevent death?"

So, what are some helpful, and wholly Buddhist approaches to comforting a person who is ill?

We should both keep in mind and remind others that the body is impermanent, yet we should not ignore the body or despise it.

Simply because the body is subject to decay, disease, and death does not mean we can ignore our health. We can't simply engage in unhealthy practices using the excuse of an impermanent body.

Even though the stated goal of Buddhism is the elimination of the cycle of birth and death, it does not mean we can devalue life. So, here we are instructed both as a point of comfort to others as well as an admonition to ourselves that it is incumbent upon us to make consistent effort to maintain our health. Which further means to work in harmony with the advice of skilled doctors, i.e. take your medicine, follow guidelines for activity, diet and so forth. When under the care of a doctor, you have an important partner in your health care and it is a team effort.

The body – being material and subject to decay, disease and death – will experience suffering and pain. It can be helpful to discuss this in an open and honest conversation. Talking about the nature of the pain, the limitations the pain is causing, the methods available for minimizing the pain, and how to transform the suffering caused by pain. Vimalakirti admonishes that in this conversation the goal is not to seek the Nirvana of Hinayana Buddhism, which teaches that the ultimate goal of practice can only be achieved at death. We should not encourage such an escapist attitude.

Escaping pain and suffering has become the default practice of many doctors and as a consequence we have an opioid epidemic that is taking the lives of thousands of people. I myself witnessed the effects of over prescribing pain medications when I worked in a hospital inpatient detox unit. The potential for abuse of the powerful pain medications is far greater than the benefit.

Rather than steering patients to other pain-reducing modalities, doctors simply prescribe a pill. Not only does this frequently lead to addiction, even in patients who follow instructions, it also leads to a mentality of not being willing to try non-medicated solutions to pain management such as meditation, acupuncture, acupressure, massage therapy and others.

Escape, whether through medication or unhealthy religious ideations, is not the solution, and Vimalakirti discerned this thousands of years ago. We ignore this at our peril.

We don't often think about ego when we think of illness and suffering, yet for the sick person it is frequently all about ego. The mind focuses sharply on self. Sometimes that focus is so intense that others and their needs are ignored. Sometimes this may cause the patient to seem demanding, or inconsiderate. It's tough to endure this as a caregiver.

The ego is a function of the mind. The body, Vimalakirti says, is without ego. In illness, the body is overruling the mind, and it is important to remind the patient of this. Helpful to this goal is to encourage the patient to teach others. I would add that Vimalakirti is speaking from a Buddhist perspective and the assumption is that the ill person will teach Buddhism. However, this concept of the patient teaching others can be applied to all sorts of aspects of the disease process. This is why support groups can play a beneficial role in disease comfort, not only for the patient but also for the caregivers.

Patients frequently resist participation in support groups, saying there is nothing they need to hear from others. What they overlook is the benefit of sharing and helping others. I've written before that the shortest path out of the Four Lower Worlds of Hell, Hunger, Animality, and Anger is to strive for the realm of Humanity. The restorative and healing and pain-reducing benefit of helping others is amazing. When we can, even just a little bit, shift our focus from ourselves to others it has tremendous impact on our suffering and pain.

Many who deliver medical care and caregivers must travel the fine line between remembering the emptiness of the body and dwelling upon its final extinction. How can you be honest without being forlorn or causing hopelessness? Vimalakirti saw this difficulty and cautioned that being dishonest about the disease or illness causes harm; being brutally honest causes harm. There is no one answer.

How challenging it is to deliver the news of the unexpected amputation of a leg, especially to someone who was vital and active only hours before. It is unimaginable, and yet the news is unavoidable. Telling someone that their life will never be the same again, or that they will probably die soon, is a difficult message to bear and to hear.

When I was taking care of young boys during the beginning of the AIDS epidemic, I met and cared for some truly heroic people. I've told this before in other books and said it numerous times in presentations, yet I can't help but tell it again and again. A boy who had always wanted to play trumpet yet never got around to it, when given one week before death managed to blast out terribly off-key notes that rivaled any symphony composed by any great musician. How noble it is to choose who you will be when you die.

To wish to die clean and sober, when by all rights you could certainly be excused for using drugs or alcohol, is still something I am moved by. It was important to many of those young boys not to die an addict, not to die an alcoholic. Yes, some might say well they were only clean or sober for a short while, yet that short while for most was hell. They chose to elevate their lives out of suffering even if they could not eliminate the pain and futility.

I don't know how they did it. I am not sure I could have done as they did. They had no support, other than my presence and my witness. Most had been abandoned by friends and family. Certainly, society had forgotten them. They taught me so much, and I hope to be a good bearer of their life stories. These boys knew they were going to die, they were going to die alone, they were going to be forgotten, yet they felt from some deeper place in their being that they were the ones in charge of how they would live and die in all of that.

The last time I saw the AIDS quilt it had grown so large that the whole thing could no longer be displayed in one place. To walk along and read the memorial squares with stories in words and pictures was a truly heart-wrenching experience, one I'll never forget. The boys' lives I witnessed, the stories they lived, were only a small fraction of the number of times these same types of stories were repeated. I remember one boy who wanted to learn to speak Spanish and did actually manage some phrases before he died. It may seem trivial, but nothing is trivial when you are dying.

Think about that: These young boys had days and weeks. They knew death was certain and soon, and they chose to live. How many of us forget we are going to die, ignoring our own death sentence day by day as if forever was a gift we would receive?

The body is relatively inconsequential when you come right down to it. It is what we do with that body that makes it of value. Life is truly precious, that we have by the very fact I am writing this, and you are reading it. But your lived life, your story, how you fill your days, that is of consequence.

Vimalakirti advises us to remind the ill of their harmful past actions so these are not repeated but not to either simply consign them to the past or ignore their valuable lessons in the present and into the future.

Back at the beginning of the AIDS epidemic no one knew how the disease was spread. Instead, there were all sorts of wild stories. In providing care I engaged in what would be called risky behavior. Handling blood- and puss-soaked towels without gloves is not a practice you will see in a hospital today. I had no choice. I'd rewash any old rag. That was all that was available. Who had money to buy new dressings much less sterile ones? I certainly did not. Lending my shaver and then using it again carried certain risks. Being a nail biter and having bloody cuticles and hangnails meant I had open wounds. Breathing the same air was thought by some to be a way the disease spread.

Now we know how HIV and many other communicable diseases are spread. What do we do with that information? Many choose to follow safe best practices, yet many still engage in risky behaviors. Humans will walk both sides of that street for as long as humans exist. We are ultimately responsible for all our actions, and we have the capacity to learn from our past actions, even if we don't have the necessary internal what-ever-it-is to live differently.

Not facing the realities of our behaviors is not the same as turning those past behaviors into a weapon by either the patient or caregiver. Yes, mistakes were made, and they cannot be undone. While the past is truly past, the effect of that past lingers, and the lessons of that past can be acted upon. The past is not, nor should it ever become, a weapon.

Vimalakirti comes back again to the message of reminding the patient how they can benefit others from their situation. This is again turning the illness into a teaching to eliminate the suffering of others. I know that I stated in the beginning that the illnesses being focused upon in this book were not those taken on for the purpose of instruction, but what I am saying here is that the illness should be examined for the lessons the patient can learn and then share with others. Again, this is first residing in forbearance and then stepping into the realm of humanity and lifting others up out of their suffering.

When I worked as a chaplain, what I disliked hearing the most, either from patients or caregivers, were such things as, "I don't have it as bad as some" or "compared to others I've a lot to be thankful for." It is not healthy to base one's assessment of one's life on the misery of others. I wish people could eliminate these self-harming phrases from their thinking.

It is possible to be happy without others being unhappy. It is possible to be sad without others being sadder. It is possible to be in pain and others to be in pain also. There are many possibilities where you do not need to diminish your experiences. There are many ways of being without devaluing your feelings or your life, or others. Your feelings and experiences are real, important, and worthy of you. They are your story, even if not your whole story.

Vimalakirti says that we should remind the ill bodhisattva of the great fortune they have created and experienced through their religious practice and in the face of the reality they are currently experiencing not to give way to gloom or worry.

Before I close out this section on Vimalakirti I should write a bit more about nirvana and ego as taught in this sutra. The idea of nirvana is part of a dualistic belief in that it is opposed to self or I. Both nirvana and self are empty of themselves; neither has a fixed nature or characteristics. The proper approach in Mahayana Buddhism is they are both equal and one is not to be sought over the other. This, Vimalakirti says, is the path to the elimination of dualism. We should instead be in the state of both self and nirvana as being equal and put forth our effort in striving for Anuttara-samyak-saṃbodhi, this is the liberation of expedient means with wisdom.

The Vimalakirti Sutra says:
"...the Law has nothing to do with idle theorizing. To declare that one must recognize suffering, renounce attachments, realize how to reach extinction, and practice the Way, is mere idle theorizing, not seeking the way."[1]
I highly recommend the reading of this rather short sutra. Written from the voice of a lay practitioner it offers great insight into understanding and practicing Buddhism from a practical perspective.

---

1   Vimalakirti Sutra, translated by Burton Watson, Columbia University Press, 1997, page 75

6

Medicine King Bodhisattva

Deciding how to write about the bulk of Chih-i's section in the Mo-Ho Chih-Kuan has been complicated. There is much in his work that is important, especially given his role in collecting, systematizing, and disseminating the full body of Chinese medicine available during his time. He is often referred to as the father of Buddhist medicine and, in fact, Nichiren referred to him as the emanation of Medicine King Bodhisattva.

Medicine King Bodhisattva appears in Chapter XXIII, titled "The Previous Life of Medicine King Bodhisattva" of the Lotus Sutra. The chapter opens with Star-King-Flower Bodhisattva saying to the Buddha: "World-Honored One! Why does Medicine-King Bodhisattva walk about this Saha-World?" In Chih-i's travels to various centers of learning and from collecting information from visitors to his mountain temple, Chih-i gathered together a huge storehouse of medical wisdom and practice of his time.

In this chapter of the Lotus Sutra devoted to the story of Medicine King Bodhisattva, the Buddha says:

"All living beings will be able to fulfill their wishes by this sutra... just as a patient who finds a physician."

"Anyone who hears especially this Chapter of the Previous Life of Medicine King Bodhisattva also will be able to obtain innumerable merits. …When he obtains this truth, his eyes will be purified. With his purified eyes he will be able to see seven billion and two hundred thousand million nayuta Buddhas or Tathagatas, that is as many Buddhas as there are sands in the River Ganges."

"I will transmit this Chapter of the Previous Life of Medicine King Bodhisattva to you. Propagate this chapter throughout the Jambudvipa in the later five hundred years after my extinction lest it should be lost, and lest Mara the Evil One, the followers of Mara, gods, dragons, yaks, and kumbhandas should take advantage of the weak points of the people of the Jambudvipa.

"…this sutra is a good medicine for the diseases of the people of Jambudvipa. The patient who hears this sutra will be cured of his disease at once. He will not grow old or die."

Repeatedly in this chapter, the Buddha tells Star-King-Flower about the merits and superiority of the Lotus Sutra. In seven different ways the Buddha extols the superiority of the Lotus Sutra: "More honorable than the other sutras", "father of all the sages and saints", "superior to any of the other sutras expounded either by Tathagatas or by Bodhisattvas or by Sravakas", "superior to any other sutra" are a few of the superlatives given to the Lotus Sutra and leave no doubt about the intent of the Buddha that this Sutra is indeed the most efficacious teaching for all the inhabitants of the Saha world.

Chih-i is most widely known as the great compiler and systematizer of Buddhism and the teachings of the Buddha, which entered China from Pakistan, Afghanistan, and India. This was a haphazard process complicated by physical barriers such as the Himalayas and by the various languages and cultures from which the sutras were transmitted. The Lotus Sutra itself is influenced greatly by the emerging merchant class and the impact of trade along the Silk Road. We see this in various parables told in the sutra. There is even architectural evidence to suggest that the compound of the father in the parable of the Burning House was more representative of Afghan than India. Chih-i, though, not only systematized the cannons of Buddhism, he also did the same for Buddhist medicine and traditional Chinese medicine.

The section of the Mo-Ho Chih-Kuan dealing with Contemplation on Disease offers very detailed instructions on how to diagnose and treat various diseases. I struggled the most with this information, not because of its complexity, but whether it is appropriate for this book and for the casual reader. My chief concern is the tendency of people to self-diagnose and self-medicate. These are tendencies that the readers of Chih-i's writings would not even consider, knowing full well that these matters are best left to professionals, professionals who have fully studied and trained with others skilled in the use of these traditional therapies.

This book is not intended to be a self-help medical book. Rather the purpose is to offer guidance, based on Buddhism, in how to live in the presence of disease, what our practice can bring to our lives in disease, what we can gain or lose from our lives in disease, and how to attain enlightenment in disease.

Returning again to Medicine King Bodhisattva chapter where the Buddha says: "Star-King-Flower! Anyone who aspires for, and, wishes to attain Anuttara-Samyak-Sambodhi, should offer a light to the stupa of the Buddha by burning a finger or a toe."

As I consider this I kept wondering about how it would be possible to burn oneself without catching fire? The fire and burning I come up with is that of passion. When I think about the work of medical providers and compassionate caregivers, I recall the many dedicated and passionate individuals I have met and worked with over the years. These people have been truly passionate about their work. And yes, in some cases their passion did cause them to burnout, did cause them to self-combust.

If you have ever cared for someone who is ill, and especially if it is a long-term illness for which recovery either never comes or comes after a lengthy period, then you know that the toll is great. It takes dedication, passion even if unaware that it is a passion, to care for the sick. And without proper care it can be completely consuming.

When reading of Gladly-Seen-By-All-Beings Bodhisattva burning his arms and the Bodhisattvas, gods, men, asuras and others becoming overcome with sorrow, I immediately think of the sorrow families express when a loved one or a friend becomes ill. They are full of sorrow and sadness, wondering, "What can we do?" Doctors and nurses who have witnessed numerous tragedies still cry, even if only in their hearts, when they must treat the sick and especially if the situation is hopeless, just as all were overcome with sorrow over Gladly-Seen-By-All-Beings' loss of his arms.

People don't often think about the deaths of hospital clinicians, nurses, aides, and doctors, yet the hospital family does. When a beloved and caring team member dies it hits all with tremendous impact. Frequently these deaths are from what could be termed job-related stress – heart attacks, suicide and automobile accidents that may be related to overwork. The stress of any care provider, whether in a facility setting or at home, is often overlooked or ignored.

Not only is there the stress of the emotional impact there is the workload stress. In a care facility there are always more patients and needs than staff. The same is true at home. The hours are long in both a care facility and at home, although at home there may never be any time off. The resources are always insufficient and stretched thin.

Passion and dedication are what gets you through.

One of the last young boys I took care of before I moved from San Diego was a particularly hard case for me. I had been taking care of this guy for several weeks. His infections were almost unspeakable; the worst I'd ever witnessed. It was a constant battle of puss and blood. I swear I don't know how he managed to live as long as he did.

Right before he died, an AIDS ward at the hospital finally opened and he managed to get one of the five beds. I had been working almost round the clock on my printing job. In fact, the evening I last saw him I had come off a 36-hour shift. I was exhausted. I stopped by the hospital on my way home and sat with him in his room.

It was the first time I can say he had been comfortable since before he became sick. In the hospital, he was in a clean bed. The best I had been able to do was wash the linens, and they never came clean from the blood no matter how I tried. His hospital bed linens were all white, and his gown clean. The room was well lit, and I guess he had some decent food. I couldn't always provide the best meals, what with my own meager money, though he always had something to eat.

I sat in the chair and I drifted off to sleep there in front of him. When I woke up a little while later, he looked at me and said: "Why don't you go home now. You're tired, and I'm alright." I said that was a good idea and left. Shortly after I got home the hospital called to say he had died.

As sad as that was I didn't have time to really grieve because I then needed to make arrangements for his burial. It fell to me and my partner and one other person to come up with the money to have him cremated and buried. The day we buried him his mother showed up. We had told his grandmother of his death because he was close to her. His mother had kicked him out and "disowned" him. She showed up at the cemetery and asked us where he had been living because she wanted to get his things and sell them. We refused to tell her.

In some ways I think I am still grieving his death.

"I shall be able to obtain the golden body of the Buddha because I gave up my arms," Gladly-Seen-By-All-Beings Bodhisattva declares. I think of the many golden body Buddhas I witnessed over the years who, through their passion, not only gave up their arms but their legs, their minds and their lives doing the compassionate acts of caring for the sick. "If my words are true and not false, I shall be able to have my arms restored." And these caregivers time after time continued to return to their passion of care.

One night I was the on-call chaplain and was notified that an Adult Trauma Code Level One was being brought into the hospital. A Level One trauma means that there is at least one person from all the disciplines in the hospital present and attending the admission and emergency room treatment.

The role of the chaplain in all of this is loosely defined and usually up to the individual chaplain to determine. The way I defined mine was to notify the person recording all the events in the room of who I was and that I was the chaplain. Then I would stand off to the side behind the persons who would be providing the actual medical treatment. The space is very small for what needs to be done.

Once I checked in and stood out of the way, I chanted in my head and witnessed the efforts the skilled professionals made to try to revive a male pedestrian who had been struck by a motor vehicle. I constantly chanted and as doctors and nurses gave blood, various fluids, injections to try to chemically kick-start the heart or to boost the heart rate. They worked in shifts giving chest compressions and pumping a breathing bag.

This went on for quite a while but all to no avail. When a doctor finally called the man's time of death, I witnessed something I had never seen happen before. Rather than everyone moving on to the next patient, the next trauma, everyone hung around. They were hugging each other and crying. I could see their shoulders shake and the bodies tremble. After a while they began to wipe their noses and go about the business of the emergency department.

As a few of them were finishing up the paperwork and reports I asked about the scene I had just witnessed. I've written about this event before, yet as a witness I will tell the story again about Chilly

Willie. He was a homeless man, a street person. He was what they called a frequent flier, meaning he would appear in the ER once or twice a month to get something treated. The ER was his personal physician, as it is for many homeless and poor.

About 10 years before his wife had been struck and killed by an automobile. Before that, Chilly Willie had been what society would call normal. He had a job and a place to live – all the things used to measure normality. Then when his wife died, it all fell apart. He lived on the streets and all such a life entails. Recently he had begun to turn his life around and was about to get his own place again. The Emergency Department staff were seeing him less and when he did come, he showed signs that he was managing his health care. You can tell these things.

They deeply cared for this person society had cast aside. Society had no place for a man who was deeply traumatized by the death of his wife. Society only had space for him as a homeless person, nameless to most. The folks, the Medicine King Bodhisattvas in the ER, knew him. He was a real person to them, and they mourned his life and his death.

7

Managing Illness

In Chih-i's time, and in fact for most of the time humans have been around until more recent times, the idea of living with long-term illness didn't exist much. You either recovered or you died. With the advances of modern medicine people are living longer, dying at later ages, and living with illnesses that would have previously meant death.

This is a wonderful benefit of modern medical science. We have much to be thankful for. We also have much to think about that often goes without thought. Living with illness, living with diseases, is complicated and medical treatments making it possible to live in such conditions do not often take into account the challenges presented to us as families, caregivers, institutions, insurance and so on.

For the remainder of this book I am going to change slightly the wording that comes from Chih-i. Rather than "cure," I'll use words such as "manage," or "live with." I'd like it to be manage, and maybe my very good editors, John and Mary Hughes, will assist me in continuity and conformity.

My reason is as stated above. Death or cure are no longer the only options in illness. The other option is living with the illness, however that may look. Most of the time we are very eager to live. At least until the life given to us becomes unmanageable, and we are kept alive by the medicine and medical treatments. I won't veer into the assisted suicide debate. That would be out of place here. Yet medical care in long-term illness is a real and serious issue. What happens to the elderly parent who can live with some serious physical ailments yet has no one to care for them and so ends up in a care facility, and then the care they get isn't always the best care they need? These are serious medical issues people face every day.

Also, since I am not a doctor I don't want people to misuse what I offer in this book and think what is written can be considered cures for anything other than the sufferings of illness and not the illness itself. I don't think I can emphasize this enough given the tendencies of people to try to administer their own self-discovered medical curatives.

I firmly stand behind the practice that Nichiren followed: When he was sick, he sought out the most skilled medical expert he knew. Shijo Kingo provided prescriptions and advice for the treatment of Nichiren's illnesses. Nichiren certainly had available to him the writings of Chih-i and could have read the instructions contained within, yet he knew that true wisdom lay in going to the professionals who have trained in such things. Nichiren's practice of seeking medical help was also his guidance to his followers who became ill. He didn't try to practice medicine; his practice was Buddhism.

So please, if you are sick take it seriously and seek professional help. Whether the illness is of the body or of the mind, seek out professionals. Consider what you may find in this book as perhaps supplemental information from a Buddhist perspective to assist in your faith as you live through your illness.

Please hear me, always seek professional help.

8

Religious Ideation

Faith can be a wonderful thing, but it can also be dangerous. I'll write more about the power of faith with regard to managing illness and disease. For now, I would briefly like to pause and speak of harmful religious ideation, a term frequently used among chaplains when working with patients and families who believe something harmful to their lives and contrary to the advice of their medical providers.

As Nichiren Buddhists, we chant the Odaimoku, Namu Myoho Renge Kyo, and we believe in the power of that phrase in our lives. It is not a magic incantation, though. Even Nichiren only attributed the extra years of his mother's life to proper medical advice from Shijo Kingo and his own faith and practice of the Lotus Sutra. This is an encouraging statement from the founder of our school of Buddhism, that with proper medical advice, care, and treatment coupled with firm faith he was able to prolong his mother's life by seven years.

He was not able to prevent her eventual death, and I know of no instance where he even suspected that he would be able to do so. Even with the power of Odaimoku he was not without doubt that he might die on Sado Island or that he wouldn't succumb to the rigors of life on Mount Minobu. He was always frank in speaking of the hardship and struggle of living, and we might say he was the most ardent believer and practitioner of the Lotus Sutra.

I don't believe he doubted the benefit of chanting the Odaimoku but that he realized being a human meant the eventual decay and death of the body. Odaimoku is not a magic phrase meant to replace skillful living and skillful means for caring for this fragile body.

To live is to die.

Hearing someone say, "All you have to do is chant and have faith and you can overcome anything," is not always helpful. There are some illnesses, some karma, that we may not be able to overcome, and perhaps all we can do is minimize or mitigate or lessen the impact.

When we offer such "overcome anything" advice, what we fail to consider is that if a person is not able to eliminate or cure an illness or overcome a situation, then we subject them to doubts about their self-worth or their faith. This can lead someone to think they don't have faith when in fact they do.

We simply do not know the trajectory of a person's life. We can be the best support when we can be in the present with them, be aware of their suffering, and agree to walk with them in a non-judgmental capacity as a friend who will be with them no matter what.

I have been with patients whose illness has been compounded with guilt that they have done something wrong or that their faith isn't good enough or that they have received divine punishment of some sort. These feelings strongly impact in a negative way the curative the medical providers are offering.

I will write more of the power of faith and belief to impact a person's health in both negative and positive ways. Our faith in the Lotus Sutra and our chanting the Odaimoku attunes our life to the truth of the universe. This truth is that all sentient beings are equal and have an equal potential to manifest Buddha nature in their lives in accord with their life form, their power, their nature, and so on through the Ten Aspects or Ten Suchnesses. As sentient beings who inhabit a material life, we are all equally subject to the cycle of birth, growth, old age, sickness, decay, and death. As co-participants in this miracle of life and death we as Buddha can be acutely aware that all beings, ourselves included, have this potential for suffering and our faith can guide us and enable us to guide others in how to eliminate suffering even while not eliminating pain and loss.

In 1971, I was stationed at the Marine Corps base Kaneohe, Hawaii. In that year I had a significant pain and swelling in my knees. It was so bad I could hardly walk. I went to the Marine sick bay, and the doctors sent me to Trippler Army Hospital on the other side of the island. It was determined after many doctor visits and consultations that I was suffering from significant scar tissue from my knees being fractured while in boot camp some three years earlier.

I was prescribed a rigorous regimen of physical therapy. Now physical therapy then meant that every day I had to show up at sick bay and perform the required exercises and whirlpool treatments. There was no getting out of it; no slacking off. I was assigned to light duty, with no prolonged standing, no marching, and no kneeling or squatting. After six months, there was no improvement, and it was decided that surgery to remove the knee caps and replace them with plastic ones was the only option.

When I shared this with my leaders and others in the Soka Gakkai, the Japanese women became quite alarmed, as was I. Synthetic knee caps, with their limited lifespan, would mean that I would be doomed to a life of constant knee problems.

Immediately they did whatever was necessary to secure for me a gofu, a special "medicinal" piece of paper that is to be eaten. This paper purportedly was a snippet of the paper that was used to clean the surface of the large Gohonzon, located at the head temple of the Nichiren Shoshu in Taisekiji. The instructions were that I had to chant 1 million Odaimoku before consuming it. So, the special gofu was placed on the main altar at the community center and in one month I completed the 1 million Odaimoku.

I still fondly and warmly recall the many nights I would stay at the community center chanting to the Gohonzon in the dark after everyone had left for the evening. The old community center had a koi pond that wrapped around the building with several waterfalls. Since the temperature there is quite mild the windows would be open and I would chant to the sound of the water and the insects of the night.

I would fall asleep, wake up, chant some more and sleep. Chanting is practically all I did. I wasn't panicked or worried. I felt quite serene and confident that all would work out for the best. I had by this time developed a sense of practice that worrying about something wasn't necessary although appropriate actions were always required.

After that month of 1 million Odaimoku I finally took the gofu along with the water from the altar. I remember my disappointment at not feeling anything magical – no lights, no special goose bumps. It was all quite ordinary, other than the fact of eating paper.

My next appointment at the hospital was to be with five surgeons who were going to make final review of my knees and set the date for the surgery. Prior to that meeting I had a final set of X-rays done. I already knew that there had been a significant improvement in my knees. The swelling had gone away, and the pain had left as well. The result of the consult was that surgery would not be needed, and that I was to be returned to full duty with a notation of service-related injury.

Now, I don't know exactly what happened. Yes, one could say that the Odaimoku and the gofu "cured" my knees. Yet I've always been hesitant to say that. One reason I am reticent to simply attribute it to the gofu and Odaimoku is the tendency of people then to oversimplify it and think that the outcome will be the same for them if they do this "magical" thing.

Odaimoku and our Buddhist practice cannot be reduced to a simple reliance on some outside miraculous phenomena. There is, at the core of it, all our own effort and our own faith and those are not easy things. It was, I believe, a combination of the marshaling of my inner faith and my inner healing resources, my practice, the dedication to do the best for my body and soul, the attention I received from the compassionate Japanese women, the support I received from the Sangha, the medical treatment and care of the military medical providers. It was a whole bunch of things and lacking any one of them the outcome may have been entirely different.

There have been studies done recently which indicate that in many instances the cure for many of our illnesses actually begins when we make the call to schedule an appointment with a doctor. There is evidence that even the act of visiting the doctor is more the ending of the illness than the beginning of treatment. In my case the process was six months long. Did the resolution begin at the beginning of that period or did it begin when I consumed the gofu or was it both? I simply do not know. I do know that nothing worked against the other.

Perhaps the chanting and the gofu combined to marshal my inner healing abilities in a way that simple positive thinking could not. Perhaps I had such faith in the gofu and the Odaimoku that I didn't have in the physical therapy. I'm not sure.

So, while I caution about harmful religious ideation I do want to leave open the possibility of helpful religious ideations as well.

9

Power of Names

In my leisure I read a lot of science fiction, fantasy, general fiction, and young-adult literature. When reading anything dealing with magic, or sorcery, or witchcraft and lore, one thing that is constant is the power of a name. In fact, mages, witches, and sorcerers guard their true name knowing that someone who knows their name has power over them.

Think about this in regard to your own name. While this may not feel true for you, I suspect that when someone mispronounces your name you almost immediately, perhaps reflexively, correct them, even if you follow it quickly with forgiveness for the slight.

When working in a hospital, you run across lots of names, and especially with a growing immigrant population the names can be very different from the usual Anglo-Saxon names that were so prominent as I was growing up. I always felt it was important to try my best to pronounce someone's name correctly. When I would struggle, people would sometimes try to ease my burden by saying, "It's alright," or "That's good enough," which, in my mind, discounted the value of their very important identification, their name.

My last name is Jeffus, and it is interesting how difficult that seems to be for people to pronounce. Often though, it is because they are trying to insert letters in there to make it be a different name.

Jeffers is one of the most frequent versions. I'll be honest here. My preference is that it be pronounced correctly, though I will usually accept any bastardization that the person is finally able to say. Several years ago, I legally changed my first name to Ryusho. That is a difficult name for people to wrap their minds around. I usually give them a hint to ignore the "y" since they won't be able to pronounce it anyway. The difference in sound is subtle and, for non-Japanese speakers, is exceedingly difficult without practice. Still, my internal preference is that it come close.

Perhaps you're not like that. However, I have found most people prefer that their name is pronounced correctly.

What's this got to do with contemplating disease? When we know the name of something, this helps us to feel as if we have some "power" over the thing. When I was living in Japan I was nicknamed "nan to iu'n desu ka," which means roughly, "What is this called?" It was important for my communication survival to know the name of things, so I could have some power over my environment, or at least not be completely helpless.

People feel comforted when the doctor gives them a diagnosis and a name for their illness. I used to feel that way too, and I'll get to why I don't find it so comforting now.

"Well at least I know what I have" can be comforting. It is also a form of validation that the symptoms are identifiable, known and understood. I can now say I have this illness with this particular name. For example, I have a condition of an extremely runny nose that sometimes flows and flows uncontrollably. The condition has a name, rhinitis, and for a brief moment in time when the doctor told me that, I felt relieved. It was sort of an "Ah ha" moment.

But then I got to thinking about it and wondered whether I had been reduced to a small entry in some medical text on page 694 of volume 2? Am I not more than that? Does this mean the doctor now quits listening to me because he has filed me away in some medical jargon file cabinet? Sometimes it feels that way.

I have witnessed the relief that can quite visibly flood over a patient's face when they learn the name of their illness, even when the name is dreadful and there is no cure. I understand how having a name is very comforting on one hand. I also understand and have witnessed and experienced how convenient it is to then dismiss the individual for the disease.

One thing taught to chaplains, and something I had learned working with AIDS patients, is that the disease does not define the person, though the person can certainly live a life defined by the illness. You simply don't walk into a hospital room and say, "good afternoon Mr. Pancreatic Cancer," or "good morning, Ms. COPD." Yet I have been present in consultations and even had in my own experience a doctor jump quickly from greeting to disease, completely skipping the important middle person – the patient – in the process.

While knowing the name of one's illness is comforting, it can also become a dismissive shorthand label. "Ah, Mr. Asthma, I know everything there is to know about you. Never mind how you are feeling, and your symptoms, I know your illness, and I am the master of your treatment." Or so it seems sometimes when listening to doctors or even television commercials.

In your daily life, and especially when caring for others with illness, avoid becoming a label and avoid putting labels on others that can minimize their lives.

I spent a great deal of time working in the cardiac ICU and understood much of the medical jargon, purpose of treatments and reasons for certain drugs and what they are expected to do. One of the functions I felt it important to serve was to keep it human and keep it patient-related. That is, yes, all of these symptoms are present and certain treatments and protocols are appropriate, but beneath all of that there is a human being who may be suffering. Are we communicating with that person or are we communicating with their illness?

From years working with geriatric patients, I know many of the illnesses that beset the elderly. I know many of the common symptoms, the side effects of the medications used, and what it looks like when a patient is "non-compliant." But none of those things are the patient. Not every person experiences the same thing, and not everything that appears as non-compliant is indeed non-compliance. Not every person wanting pain relief is "drug-seeking."

The patient is a person and the person may be experiencing certain symptoms. Here's the critical thing in contemplating disease: Remember that you are more than a particular named illness; and your symptoms are uniquely your own, not those written in a medical text.

Listen to yourself. It is even helpful to record your medical experiences. The mind has a funny way of distorting your perception of reality.

Some of you may know that I am an avid keeper of a journal or notebook. It's more than a journal; it is everything from shopping lists to notes about sunrise to what I bought at the grocery store and how much I paid. One thing it does contain is notes about my general health.

Currently I am dealing with a recurrence of a muscle spasm in my buttocks, piriformis. Walking and sitting and anything short of laying down is very painful. This debilitating condition causes stress because I can't do the things that are important to me and add quality to my life. I'm not taking it lying down, though. I'm fighting back.

As I write this it has been one month now that the pain has been so great I can hardly walk. Sometimes I need a cane to simply stand up. I have found that if I sit on a heating pad and use a TENS (transcutaneous electrical nerve stimulation) unit, I can then walk on flat ground for about 30 minutes and not very far. Since where I live is very hilly, I get in my car with the dog and drive over to the large parking lot and field in one of the neighborhood churches and walk on the level ground until it becomes unbearable. Little by little, it is getting better.

When I get discouraged, I sometimes think it has been going on nearly forever. And that is how it can seem. Yet when I look at my journal, I can see some progress, even amid the ups and downs, and that it has only been one month. The first time I had this problem I suffered with it for seven months, but I survived and got better. So, the journal helps me not to become despondent.

Keeping a journal is also good medical advice because you have a record when you talk to your doctor about your health. Without a journal record and only a vague recollection of symptoms when you visit your doctor, it is easy for the doctor to fill-in the blanks with medical text symptoms, reducing you to a page in a reference book.

However, when you go into the doctor and you can state that 50 out of the last 60 days you have had extreme difficulty doing something and you did these things and took this prescribed medicine and the results were this, all of this information keeps you real and a person and not some dismissed named illness. You maintain your humanity in the face of simplistic names. You remain the patient and not the disease.

10

Your Visit

Previously I mentioned the importance of keeping a journal of your illness experience, a medical journal. In the past I've also advocated the benefit of keeping a gratitude journal. Journaling, however you decide to do it – whether through words, drawings, collage, completely free form or a mixture – has no known harmful effects and only known beneficial effects.

It seems our brain, perhaps our whole being, is programmed to remember bad things more than good things. This may be due to the importance of knowing where that saber-tooth tiger was yesterday who killed your cave-mate. It's important to remember where those poisonous berries were that your friend ate before he died. Knowing where danger exists is key to survival.

Gratitude journals have been shown to significantly help reduce sadness, hopelessness, and depression, as well as other common negative life effects such as stress. So, what are you thankful for today? What were you thankful for last week? What happened at the beginning of the month that you remember was a pleasant experience? What happened two weeks ago? Most people, I'm willing to bet, can't remember two weeks ago, and barely one week ago. That will certainly be the case about subtle changes in your medical wellbeing.

As we all know, the time doctors are allotted with patients has been greatly reduced, and is now on average roughly 7 minutes. That's the ideal the doctor is measured by in many cases. That's not a whole lot of time. It would be better if it were longer and it isn't likely to change anytime soon. Our choice as patients is then how to use this limited time.

First, it is important to ensure that your doctor has read your chart, your medical history or at least a summary of it before your meeting with him. He will know from the record what you complained about last time. It's usually worded something like patient presents as follows, or patient complained about this. It won't be word for word; it will be a summary of what they felt was important from your last visit. You may wonder how they do that if they are so busy.

During the visit they may or may not scribble some notes, but after their visit they go to their computer or the doctor charting area and dictate the interaction verbally into the computer or a transcription service. They can speak faster than they can type and it makes it very efficient. The voice memo is then transcribed by a service and put into your record. Occasionally the chart notes are indeed text entered by the doctor, though usually this is done primarily in fast-paced situations such as emergency room visits. This is not a fixed rule and it can and does vary greatly.

The point is, there is record the doctor has looked at. You don't need to bring up your last visit again. You may spend your limited time with the doctor going over the same things, that is your choice, but it isn't necessarily the most efficient use of your time with the person you expect to diagnose and treat your illness. Certainly, if there is something new, bring it up. That's what you are there for.

In the last hospital where I worked every patient was given a wire-bound journal and a pen. The purpose was to record events in the hospital, experiences such as whether you liked the food, the nurses, the environmental services people – anything and everything. Most important, it was so you and your family or friends could share their concerns about your health with the attending physicians and nurses.

Now if you think the short window of time available to you in a doctor's office is bad, then consider in the hospital you will often have even less time. Also, whereas in a doctor office visit you know when it will happen, in the hospital you may not know. And it may happen when your family or care-provider is not present. Keeping the journal is a good idea because when that doctor or resident visits you can get right to your questions. You can then write them down and the answers in order to keep track of what has been said and what you expect for your treatment and so forth. It can serve as a valuable memory aid.

When the family shows up and you are tired or simply excited to see the grandkids, you don't need to worry about whether you are forgetting something the doctor told you. When you are bombarded with questions by family you can simply answer them with ease from your journal and don't need to struggle with trying to remember everything. It can also serve as a check on whether you have received the things you were expecting, such as diagnostic tests or medications. You may have thought that today you were going to have a brain scan and you notice nothing seems to be going in that direction. You can then mention it to your nurse, who may not have been told. Or perhaps you misunderstood, or perhaps the doctor re-evaluated things and changed his mind and the word did not filter back to you. These things do happen and that journal by your bedside can help keep it all sorted.

Here I've been talking a lot about doctor/patient interactions, yet this is equally true and applicable to care-providers in the home, such as family and friends or even hospice providers. Knowing what worked two days ago or what didn't work two days ago is more valuable information than "I don't feel good" or "I haven't felt good in weeks."

Write down even short notes such as, "I went to take out the garbage and felt weak, and had a hard time breathing, it was 8 PM and when I came in, I had to do a nebulizer breathing treatment which after doing I could breathe much easier. The next day I felt fine though was a bit tired and slept a lot. My sleep was interrupted by difficulty breathing and I needed to us my rescue inhaler." This is all valuable and actionable information. Knowing that six out the past 10 days you needed to increase your nebulizer use beyond once a day is significant information for the doctor or caregiver and can provide the basis for further modifications in your treatment.

You are the owner of your visit with your medical provider; the question or variable is how shall you use this limited and valuable opportunity? Will you come prepared with facts and information about what you experienced, what you tried, what worked and what didn't? And speaking of what worked, this is important as well: You may forget that over the past five months there were 20 days when you randomly did such-and-such a thing and had a pleasant day, better than most. It may be so random that you didn't pay it any attention.

You think you would remember, but most people, myself included, do not. We remember what hurts, what sucks, what was disappointing, what was limiting. We don't always remember that when we got up and did such and such right away, and then did such-and-such the overall effect was a very good day. We especially don't remember it when we don't repeat it over and over. Yet keeping a journal allows us the chance to look back and discover that every time we did something a certain way we had a good result. This is huge information. This is golden. This is medicine in the modern age.

In more distant times we had a more direct connection to the village medical provider, whether herbalist, healer, shaman, or what have you. They knew us; we knew them. They knew our family. They knew us when we ran around with no clothes. They knew us when we came back from our first hunt or harvest or wove our first cloth. They knew us for our pranks, our foibles, our weaknesses, our proclivities. They knew us. They also knew when a treatment was working and when it wasn't. And often they knew this daily and could observe the changes. For better or worse, that isn't how medicine is today. This is why we, as patients, need to do our part to fill in the gaps.

If you come to the doctor visit unprepared then you are Mr. Asthma Smith, a medical condition first and an individual person second. If you come prepared, then you are Ms. Rosenthal with asthma-related symptoms and who responds more favorably to these medications and treatment plans. You have a vital role to play in your illness and it is best played when you truly contemplate and engage in your health treatment.

These may not appear to be Buddhist principles and certainly don't use a lot of Buddhist jargon, yet fundamentally they lie at the heart of our Buddhist practice of knowing ourselves, who we are, what we are, where we are.

Contemplating disease involves many aspects of Buddhist practice; knowing self is a start. Next up is Cessation. But first take these previous words to heart: become an active participant in your medical care; contemplate your illness; keep a journal.

11

Losses and Benefits

"The medicine of this secular world may cost a fortune and take time to prepare. Also, they may be bitter. Also, they may come with prohibitions, but those who rely on them for their lives continue to take them until they die. But now I present a method that does not cost a cent, does not waste even a half-a-day effort, is not bitter to the taste, and can be eaten and drunk as you wish. Nevertheless, people do not seek to practice it, and ordinary people are not aware of its value. Perhaps its charm is too high, and few can appreciate it; this causes me great distress."

This is a quote from Chih-I from the sixth century which could have been written just today. The cost of many medications prescribed for patients is in some cases so high people simply cannot afford the cure. And almost all prescriptions come with a list of possible side effects that outnumber the benefits. Not that the possible side effects will absolutely happen, but they certainly are cause for concern when taking medicines.

I've been following a Tweet thread for several days concerning prescription medications, the elderly, fall risks, and medications that conflict with one another. While this has focused on prescriptions taken by the elderly these risks are equally true and of concern for anyone taking medications. The fact is, some medications counteract each other or even cause toxicity when taken together. Some medications are to be taken with food and some without. Some medications can be taken with certain foods and not with others. Taking prescription medications is complicated and the patient may not always be equipped with enough information to keep up with all this.

One point advocated continually in this Tweet conversation is using a single provider, one pharmacy as this will enable the pharmacist to examine the medications you are currently taking and advise you about possible harmful interactions. You would think your doctor would know this, but it isn't always the case that they know your prescription history. Each time I go to the VA hospital my doctor goes over the medications I am currently taking. I'm fortunate that I have a single healthcare provider in the VA.

For many people, however, changes in insurance coverage may cause a change in their medical providers or the approved network hospital. This means that you may at some point be visiting a different doctor.

Also, a pharmacist is more specially trained in the medications that are being prescribed. Your doctor may know of some of the benefits and some of the possible side effects, but they may not be as well-versed on interactions with other medications. That is the pharmacist's specialty.

Whenever we are given a prescription medication it is important to weigh the potential for benefit alongside any possible negative consequences or potential losses and limitations from taking that medication.

Besides the pluses and minuses of various medications there are other areas to look at regarding benefit and loss. Several years ago, I had to have rotator cuff surgery on my shoulder to repair a tear. The condition was very painful.

Due to complications getting insurance approval, it took more than six months from the initial diagnosis until the corrective surgery. By that time, the muscles in my shoulder and arm had atrophied so much that I had almost no range of motion. Additionally, the joint had begun to calcify due to non-use and the bones and begun to grow together in the shoulder socket. The surgery was the most painful I have ever had, and I hope never to have it again. The surgery was bad and the six months of daily physical therapy afterward was equally bad. At first I could not lift my arm off of my stomach, where it was strapped after the surgery. Each day, the therapist would gradually lift it a little bit further while I lay there in agony. The millimeter lift felt as if he was twisting my arm behind my back.

I would come home from therapy exhausted, completely spent from the pain I was experiencing. At my job, I had to learn to do everything with my left hand – computer mouse, writing, eating everything. I was lucky my employer and insurance covered the therapy and the daily time off from work. That isn't a benefit many people have. When I think back to the situation I can think of few benefits from the problem or the solution other than it got fixed. Even to this day I can't put my seatbelt on, a right-handed operation that I assist by putting my left hand under my elbow and raising my right further to grade the belt buckle and swing it around me.

Now my brother's heart attack is a different story. It was relatively minor, caused by some arterial blockages that stents were able to resolve. He did not need any major surgery. He used the heart attack as a wakeup call to change his diet and exercise. We had always considered him 'big boned' – a little chunky but certainly not fat. Today, after several years of eating better, getting proper exercise he is competing in bodybuilding competitions in California. When I received a photo of him a few months ago, I told him it's a good thing he wasn't meeting me at the airport because I would not have recognized him. He has changed so much. So that was a clear benefit. Although it only became a benefit because of how he used the event to make decisions about his future.

Let me shift gears here a bit, still staying on loss and benefit though from a different perspective. In my time, and in every medical person's time working in a hospital, we all experience the coding of patients. Code is the jargon for a person's heart stopping. As a chaplain I always attended every code. During the day time you went to codes in your unit and at night as the on-call you went to any and all codes. When they announce a code there is a rapid response team that runs, and I do mean runs, to the event location. When that happens, you get out of the way, someone's life is depending on their arrival.

As soon as they arrive they immediately begin chest compressions. These are violent and continue until the heart starts beating or until the code is called, the patient pronounced dead. I have attended codes where, by the time they finish the patient is little more than a rag doll, their chest having been compressed so much their rib cage is shattered. Sometimes it happens ribs puncture organs, not often but it does happen. To give you an idea, a big strapping muscular guy usually only lasts not much more than 10 minutes and usually less, though it can seem like hours. They constantly rotate the person giving the compressions, it is tiring.

There is a lot of controversy about allowing family to witness this procedure because it is so violent. When I first started at the hospital in Charlotte the policy was to remove family from the room, and the chaplains or the attending nurse would do this. If I was required to do that, once I completed their removal I would return and pray outside the room. It is tough to watch this, very emotional, especially knowing the procedure and the usual outcome. Yet families and patients want it done. Now the policy is to allow the family to watch the procedure being done.

I agree with the idea of family watching it. Sometimes families have unrealistic ideas and expectations. Let me say, if you've ever taken CPR training with a dummy, you have no idea what goes on. Depending upon the body of the patient, their weight, fat, age, and so forth the patient at times literally bounces off the bed while the person doing compressions puts their entire weight into the compressions. Imagine an 180 pound person pressing their hands on your sternum with all of their weight behind that press, and then doing it several reps per minute.

One question asked of patients by medical staff and also a question on Advance Directives or Living Will is whether you want to be resuscitated. This is a standard question for anyone admitted into the hospital. If a person says yes then they are listed as full code, meaning if the heart stops then they get CPR. Now, I don't know what you may think you know about resuscitating a patient but the only place I've seen 'paddles' used is on TV – not ever in the emergency room, not ever in the patient room, not ever anyplace in the hospital. So if that's your thinking, then it's time for an adjustment.

If a person chooses not to be resuscitated then they are listed as DNR, Do Not Resuscitate. I am a DNR as well as DNI, do not intubate. When my heart stops it stays stopped. It is said that most medical professionals choose DNR, though I only know this from reading books, I never did a survey.

CPR can be a lifesaving procedure, a vital procedure, though it is in rare situations that is true. It is beyond me to list when it is good and when not, it's way more complicated than that. It is a choice everyone needs to make on their own and there are many factors as to why someone may choose one way and not another.

Let's look at my life to illustrate some of the considerations in the decision-making process. First, I am 69 years old. I've lived a good life, a full life and a life much longer than almost all my friends. I've lived almost as long as the oldest recorded person in our family history. While I'm in no rush to get out the door, I'm also not resistant to leaving. At 69, my body and bones are not as strong as they once were, though they are not as brittle as some my age. As a male my bone density doesn't decrease as rapidly as for women. Still, I've seen what the body goes through in CPR and I don't want that. I don't want to wake up with a chest so sore I can hardly breath and for which there is no pain relief.

Other considerations: I have no spouse, my partner died before me so it is just me. I am not responsible for the care of anyone other than my dog. No one depends on me to continue providing support. If I had a dependent, I am fairly certain my decision might be different depending upon other arrangements and what had been taken care of. If I had a spouse who depended upon me, my decision criteria would be different. Certainly, if I were younger, with a spouse and child or children my choice might very well be to have CPR and anything necessary to try to keep me alive.

Our life situations can and should factor into our decisions regarding our health and treatment options. To ignore them can actually be more harmful than not. This is a situation we frequently would face in the hospital where a very elderly patient is listed as full code, meaning they wanted CPR. In all likelihood if they survived the CPR they would suffer from various other complications such as broken rib bones for which nothing can be done and at an elderly age would take a long time to heal. Yet it is their choice. Sadly, many people don't fully understand what they have chosen. A spouse may not be prepared to lose their loved one and so demand CPR even though that may actually be not appropriate for their age and condition.

Another consideration is that the rate of recovery from CPR is not as great as what's portrayed on television. I think about 75% or greater survive CPR on TV. In the real world, it is less than 10%. Further, of those who are resuscitated in the real world, a very small percentage, less than 5%, live two years. My numbers may be old and I've rounded up so in all probability the percentages are worse. There are good reasons for doing CPR. They just aren't always what people expect or think about.

I would hope that as an outcome of your reading this you will consider what are your conditions for living? In a general sense, because we never know exactly what we will face, what are you willing to have done to maintain your life. For me, I have ruled out any aggressive treatments, and especially ones that would significantly reduce my quality of life. For me at this stage and age of my life I am focused on quality and not quantity.

A younger person with more life ahead and with a younger body that would heal faster, the choice may focus more on quantity, with quality of life being something to regain after recovery. There is no one right path, and it's important to consider this now rather than wait for an emergency. Further, even in an emergency you may change your mind and choose CPR. I certainly might change my mind. But I have thought about it, and I'm prepared. Most important, I am clear on my goals and values. More than anything, knowing your values, what's important and why it is important as well as what are your goals regarding your health care and why can provide you with a basis for your decisions even if they may change over time.

12

Ten Characteristics

"The medicine of this secular world may cost a fortune and take time to prepare. Also, they may be bitter. Also, they may come with prohibitions, but those who rely on them for their lives continue to take them until they die. But now I present a method that does not cost a cent, does not waste even a half-a-day effort, is not bitter to the taste, and can be eaten and drunk as you wish. Nevertheless, people do not seek to practice it, and ordinary people are not aware of its value. Perhaps its charm is too high, and few can appreciate it; this causes me great distress."[1]

This quote from Chih-i talks about a free method of managing illness, one that doesn't take much time, which can be done without any side effects, and may be taken without limit. He laments that despite all the benefits of this offering people refuse to partake.

In the Lotus Sutra parable of the Gem in the Robe we learn that the main actor has wandered around for a long time, poor, hungry, destitute, all the time not knowing of the priceless gem concealed in the hem of his robe by his friend. People walk around suffering even though within their grasp is the medicine to end all suffering. Even when told about it, they turn their backs upon it.

---

1   Swanson, Vol II, page 1348

I have seen this many times in the hospital. People are given instructions and medicines that – if followed and taken in accordance with their doctor's recommendations – would improve their lives. Instead, they do not follow directions and end up returning to the hospital within a short time. There are, of course, many reasons for this happening, some of them economic, some social, and sometimes it is because people pay attention to instructions in the hospital but at home they get ignored. These non-compliance reasons can usually be identified and addressed. The most challenging situations are when someone just simply will not do what they need to do to manage their condition.

Chih-i says that all you need are these ten characteristics: 1. Faith, 2. Utilization, 3. Diligence, 4. Constancy, 5. Distinction among disease, 6. Means, 7. Time, 8. Selecting and rejecting, 9. Protecting, 10. Know the obstacles.

FAITH

Faith is to know the Buddhist path, the first gate. Faith is belief so strong that it is invincible against the strongest enemy of faith, doubt. In this case, it doesn't mean question free. It does not mean willfully ignoring inconsistency or deliberately remaining ignorant of the dharma. This is not blind faith or faith without reason or logic. Part of faith is to question, to seek understanding and the wisdom of learning. The more we know in our faith, the stronger our faith can become.

Let me offer an explanation from my life. When I first began practicing and was faced with a personal problem, my Odaimoku was part desperation and part determination. I chanted as if I were desperate, and several times I was, and I did so with such determination that at times it was as if I was trying to bang the Odaimoku onto the Gohonzon. As I write this I am trying to come up with an image and what comes to mind is throwing grenades of Odaimoku at my problem through the Gohonzon. Remember I was in the military then.

If one grenade was good, then thousands would be better. There were times when I felt a thousand grenades would not be enough. There is a quote from Nichiren that one Odaimoku can move a mountain, and I was always searching for that one Odaimoku amid the thousands I would chant. I knew I could overcome the challenge, and I knew it took faith. But I didn't know what that was exactly, and I certainly felt I didn't have that kind of faith. It was as if I had some other kind of faith, a desperate faith.

Years later while working in the hospital I witnessed that kind of desperate faith in others of all religious beliefs. These were not people of no faith, or of weak faith. They were in a different place of desperation. It was as if they were saying, I know this belief is true, yet I am desperate enough that maybe it isn't and so I'll pray that as well. I'll pray with faith I'll pray with no faith, I'll just pray because I am desperate. That's sort of where I was.

Then over the years as I faced problems – some of the same type and some different – I noticed a change. I still knew I needed to chant abundantly and ceaselessly, but I had faith it would work out. I didn't need to have a stockpile of Odaimoku grenades. I could chant soft, gentle Odaimoku.

When I was in the Marine Corps, I faced three occasions where my Buddhist practice was threatened. The first time it happened I was very scared. In a way the situation raised the possibility of me being killed. I overcame it successfully. The second time it happened my life was directly threatened, and it also impacted my rank. I successfully overcame that as well. Finally, the third time it only affected my ability to practice freely and my rank, and this too I overcame.

As I mentioned, the first time I was very scared, the second time I was still scared but very determined. During those trials I really depended upon the moral support and encouragement of members of the Sangha. I don't think I would have succeeded and continued my practice without their support. The third time was so much different. I didn't worry about it. It was as if the persecution was happening to someone else. I chanted with an awareness of the situation but never about it or with any thought to an expectation of an outcome, good or bad.

It was a completely different experience to practice aware of the event, knowing it was there and knowing that if I simply continue doing the good things I was doing, continued with my daily practice, continued supporting the Sangha, then at the right time things would appear. I was not simply ignoring the problem and hoping it would go away. I was practicing fully aware of the situation, knowing that my faith and practice would manifest what I needed. Being afraid was not required.

This last persecution was an attempt to prohibit me from practicing Buddhism in the barracks. I was told my small altar needed to be removed from the base and I could not do my prayers out loud nor in view of anyone, something tough to do in an open bay barracks with no privacy. I refused to comply. When the time came for my court martial, the second-in-command of the squadron appeared on my behalf and said that until the squadron provided me a secure place to practice, they could not prohibit my religious practices. He also said that I was the single greatest asset to positive moral in the unit, that I always had a cheerful disposition and always helped anyone who needed it. I encouraged people. He said that it would not be in the best interest of the unit to remove the very thing that provided me the ability to be that kind of person. The charges were dismissed. I was allowed to keep my butsudan, and I was given a meritorious promotion to sergeant. Not bad. Though the rank was six months behind when I should have gotten it normally the meritorious nature looked better on my record even though I missed out on a lot of money from the delay.

Over the years the Odaimoku of desperation changed to Odaimoku of confidence and certainty. One secret to this is to realize that your idea of a solution may not be possible or even the best outcome.

When we begin chanting with a specific outcome in mind, we can easily slip into the Odaimoku of desperation and grenades.

The important thing is to have a determination that you will be able to manage this with faith and practice. I know it is natural to wonder if you have the right kind of faith, or whether your faith is strong enough. I know it happens. I certainly felt those things. If there is any way I can assure you that no matter where you think your faith is, no matter what quality you think your faith may be, it is perfect. The faith you have is the perfect faith for where you are right now. Whether it is a calm statement of "I have faith" or a through-gritted-teeth-with-much-energy "I HAVE FAITH," it is faith good enough. If you believe, then it is faith. Over time your faith changes and it happens from within so don't think you need to make it be a certain way. Don't do as I did and continually search for that one Odaimoku that will move a mountain among all the Odaimoku you chant. Chances are you chanted it yesterday anyway and didn't realize it because the mountain is still moving. That's what happened to me. The mountain moved, and it's still moving.

Utilization

While it is important to have faith, to have good medicine, to have good doctors, and to have a good treatment plan, none of that has any value unless we put them to use. The three pillars of our Buddhist practice are faith, practice, and study. Faith without practice is a three-legged stool missing a leg and will eventually topple over. It does no good to proclaim faith and fail to put that faith into daily practice.

You may have the best that current health care can provide – a good doctor, good medicine, the best facility and assistance – yet if you fail to follow the instructions, fail to take the medications, or fail to follow the recommended treatment plan, then it ought not to be a surprise that your health does not improve. And that failure of improvement cannot be laid at anyone else's feet than your own.

I was visiting with a patient one day, and we had a good conversation. She shared many things about her life, how she had become ill, the treatments she had been receiving and then sort of out of the blue she confided that she wasn't taking the medicine being given to her in the hospital. When we visit with patients our conversations are for the most part confidential, meaning what they share with a chaplain is between them and the chaplain. There are a few exceptions such as if the patient talks about self-harm, or in this case reveals that she was throwing away her medications.

After the visit, I went to the nursing station to chart my visit and to contact the physician and the patient's nurse. I explained to them what the patient told me about throwing her medicine away. The nurse said she wondered how she was doing it because she stood there to watch her take the medication. Perhaps she was holding in her mouth and then spitting it back out after the nurse left. The doctor exclaimed that it made sense. The medication should have been treating her illness, and she should have been getting better, but she was not.

She had the medicine appropriate for curing her condition, and she was not utilizing it. I expressed wonderment at her decision, but she didn't respond. She didn't share it with me why she was throwing away the medicine. The doctor and the nurse devised a strategy for ensuring her future compliance in taking her medications, and the patient was discharged shortly after this incident and showed complete recovery.

There are several possible reasons for not using effective tools in our tool box, but most of those are not well-founded and usually not in our best interest. Certainly, if we say we are Buddhists then it only seems logical for us to utilize the tools of our faith, to practice as we have been instructed, and to follow Nichiren's advice to rely on medical professionals and to couple that with our faith and practice.

Chih-i uses the analogy of taking up a sharp sword when being attacked by bandits. If you fail to use the sword, then you will not be able to repulse the bandits, and because you have the sword in your hand you will further anger them, and their attack may be more severe. We could say that this in a way corresponds to only partially taking prescription medications, especially when taking antibiotics. Failing to complete a prescribed dose of medications can cause the condition to worsen. I'll write more about this in other sections of the 10 characteristics as it overlaps several.

Diligence

Chih-i is quite strict when speaking of diligence, and my experience bears out the necessity of taking to heart in all seriousness the advice he offers. When it comes to our diligence in overcoming or living with illness there is no room to slack off. Night and day, from sunup to sunset, without rest, from the "beginning, middle, and late night to the morning," we should practice diligently. He says your sweat shows the degree of your commitment. If you try to start a fire and quit halfway, it will be difficult for you to benefit from heat.

As I have shared previously – both in example of my situation with my knee and with the persecutions I faced in the military – I chanted without rest in those situations. It is true that, as my faith grew, my Odaimoku became less of lobbing Odaimoku-grenades and more of an inner determination that my Odaimoku could be peaceful, calm, and self-assured, based upon my previous experiences. No matter where your faith is, do not spend time judging it or trying to make it conform to someone else's expression of faith. Simply chant abundantly and endlessly until you have come to a peaceful resolution, whatever that may look like. Let you and your Odaimoku meld together and be one and in harmony. If you are scared, then chant as such until you can be in peace.

Sometimes when visiting Christian patients, they would say to me, somewhat in shame, that they are so angry with God. I would often ask them, would you like to yell at God? Occasionally, I would get a chuckle. At other times, they would indeed yell at God. They usually asked me if I thought it was okay or if God would be angry.

I would often respond that from what many Christians tell me about God, s/he can handle it. S/He's a pretty big person. And besides, do you think s/he doesn't already know you're angry? You are angry. You are scared. S/He knows that. You aren't hiding anything by not admitting it. When you are in harmony, both physically and mentally, then you can shift your focus on what you need in these moments and let go of thoughts of offending God when s/he knows the offense anyway.

I wrote previously about the struggle of living with long-term illness or illness that takes a long recovery period. I offered the comparison between taking a long journey and the challenges of continued and regular practice. Diligence requires us not to be discouraged when things don't seem to be improving. No matter what, we cannot give up and allow ourselves to be defeated by Mara, the deity who creates confusion and delusion in the world.

Sometimes it is true that the best to be hoped for is a good life under new and more challenging conditions. It is also true that it may be your new reality. The temptation is to settle into a halfhearted practice founded on resignation to these circumstances. This is nothing more than Mara's army waging a war to discourage you.

During the night that the Buddha was sitting under the bodhi tree, just before his enlightenment, Mara brought his great armies and attacked the Buddha. The impression Mara was trying to create was that it was hopeless, there was no way the Buddha, as a solitary individual could defeat such overwhelming odds. This is the same as when we are looking at our health and saying it won't get better, so what's the use?

Here I am now in the elder years of my life, not as old as some who may read this but not as young as most who will read this. My body is changing. If I say failing that may sound too maudlin, yet it is certainly true. My vision is greatly diminished, and I will need cataract surgery soon. My breathing is gradually getting more difficult. My joint pains are sometimes so bad I cannot walk farther than a few houses up the block. There are good days, and there are worse days.

A friend sent me a text message out of the blue this morning. It was someone I'd not heard from since I left Charlotte. She was a good friend to me when I was in my chaplain training. One day when I had a bad experience in one of our classes and had a fairly major breakdown, she provided me great comfort and encouragement and held me as I not only dealt with the incident but with the compounded shame of falling apart. As I told her when she sent the text, some days are better than others and today is the best because I got an unexpected text from her.

My point in mentioning this is twofold. One is the reality of my life. My body will continue to decline. It won't always be bad, but I'll never be young again and never have the strength, stamina, or recuperative experiences of youth. That's not bad; it's reality. I am not sad. I'm not angry. I'm trying to live in this experience as it is without compounding it by feelings of hopelessness. The end of my life isn't now. The end of my story hasn't been written. Now is no time to give up, quit, fold my tent and roll my sleeping bag, or slack off in my faith and practice. Now, as much as ever, is the perfect time to practice. There's never been such a time as this in my life so there's lots of uncharted territory and experiences to be had. I'll take a double scoop of faith with a healthy topping of chocolate Odaimoku.

The other point in bringing up the text message is that it demonstrates the importance of checking in on people. Saying hello to friends, even if they are healthy, is so important. Think of it as your Sangha of life. Your community is both nourished by you and nourishes you. Connections are extremely critical to human health and wellbeing.

One of the major causes of death worldwide is isolation. The number of deaths attributable to isolation has risen dramatically across all age groups, all societies, and all populations. Don't take this as a negative comment about computers but a warning about computer habits and use. As more and more people replace face-to-face human contact with contact through the computer, there has been a rise in deaths related to isolation.

Much of computer interactions are based upon responding to some input made by someone else. But when we have so many online contacts and contact points we actually often have more 'friends' online than a person would have in real life. And in that quantity of friends there is a tendency for people to drop off unnoticed. Someone simply stops posting or stops connecting and the rest of the contact group continues barely missing that one person. In my online interactions I try to keep track of who I've seen posting and who I haven't seen anything from in a while. I'll send them a note saying I'm checking on them, I noticed their absence, and I hope they are doing okay. I've had more than one person say it meant so much because of all their contacts, no one had proactively reached out to them.

It isn't that people don't care. It is that the nature of the contact has changed. Because of this change it is important to try to be a bit more proactive in caring for our online contacts. You never know. You may save someone's life by letting them know someone does care even if they have never met you.

Among people with life-changing, long-term illness and especially with seniors, so much of life changes. Sometimes those changes happen so rapidly there was no chance to prepare. More often people realize that when one spouse who is elderly goes into the hospital for a long stay, there can be dramatic changes in their home life. Sometimes the previously healthy partner also becomes sick, and this really complicates returning to home. As people's lives change with illness, it becomes harder if not impossible to continue doing the things that were meaningful previously, and so you will need to find new meaningful things.

Illness can thrust a person into new and uncharted territories.

Not giving up your faith and practice and being diligent in that faith day and night is crucial not only from a faith perspective but also crucial in helping to have a bit of normalcy amid everything that is not normal. Your body will respond, and your mind will respond favorably to the returning to the touchstone of your faith. Staying diligent in your faith and practice also means remaining connected to your Sangha. Here at Myosho-ji that is one of the things I intended for our digital Sangha. It can be joined by people who may not be able to get out of there house. Of course, it's not perfect, and for people who can't use the computer it offers little, but it is more than was available to any practitioner six years or so ago.

Your life has changed; all life changes. Your routines have been altered; your old normal is not your new normal. Your faith, your practice, your reciting the sutra and chanting Odaimoku and studying the Lotus Sutra can bridge those changes. Be diligent. Or as Nichiren says in the Shoho Jisosho: "Endeavor! Endeavor!"

Constancy

Fourth of the Ten Characteristics is Constancy. By this Chih-i means that the methods we employ for living in disease or illness should all be consistent. Every thought, every effort should be focused upon our belief and actions for living in disease. It would be counterproductive for us, as believers in the Lotus Sutra and Buddhism, to employ thoughts and beliefs that contradict what we say is our core belief. As Nichiren points out in one of his letters, there is no value in mixing rice with sand. When we ascribe to the highest teachings of Buddhism as taught by the Buddha, there is no use mixing it with other less valuable or lower teachings.

This does not mean we should ignore or not seek out skillful medical providers. It would be wrong to say that only faith and practice in the Lotus Sutra is enough to overcome any illness. The Lotus Sutra teaches us in Chapter XVI that the skillful physician compounded herbs and other ingredients into a pleasing and restorative medicine to cure his sons, who had taken poison. We too need to combine the resources available to us in modern medicine with our faith and practice of the Lotus Sutra. One does not exclude the other.

Constantly keeping the Lotus Sutra foremost in our minds while following the skillful advice of medical providers is a partnership that takes place in our lives. In fact, all medical practice is a partnership between the provider and the patient. We can enhance the efficacy of the medical provider by keeping our faith foremost in our hearts and minds.

The temptation to seek solace in multiple practices – for example combining Buddhism with other belief practices – only serves to confuse the mind. The mind is important in the healing process. To grasp at various trinkets is fundamentally to believe in nothing. This may sound harsh, yet such lack of faith, hoping that one thing will work but not knowing which thing to truly believe in, diminishes the power of the mind and belief to be effective.

The convenience of the internet and the accessibility of information is both good and dangerous. It is good that we can educate ourselves about our condition. It is dangerous since it can be difficult to verify the accuracy of the information. Knowing your body, having trust in your beliefs, and skillful consultation with your medical provider all can help ensure you receive the best possible advice.

It is important always to remember that aging, bodily deterioration, health problems, and so forth are fundamentally natural. Treatments are available for many of these ailments, but treatment may not always be the best solution. This is why practicing the Lotus Sutra and knowing yourself and what is important to you and being consistent in your beliefs, your goals, and your expectations are absolutely key.

It is pointless to have your doctor provide a treatment plan that you will not commit to following. You are behaving inconsistently. It would be better to say upfront that treatment is not an option and why.

I have been advised that my trouble breathing would be greatly improved if I were to get rid of my dog. The problem is pet dander. I know this is the science, and I also know that it isn't something I can do. When my pulmonary doctor told me that his recommendation was for me to get rid of my dog, I informed him that, while I recognized the science, I also know that my quality of life would be negatively impacted. As I stated to him, for me quality is my objective in my health and not quantity.

I am being consistent in knowing what my values are for my health care. It would be inconsistent of me to expect the doctors to be responsible for quantity of life while I am only focused on quality. I also believe that animals are Buddhas too. To simply get rid of my dog would equate to my abandoning my responsibly to protect my family member. I would no more get rid of my dog than I would a child, even if the child had a communicable disease or compromised my immune system. Since I originally wrote this section my dog has died. It was a sad day to find her dead on the floor in the kitchen. Her heart finally gave out. She and I, as have all my dogs, had many good times together. Now I need to decide if I shall seek out another pet companion.

The key is to be fully aware of yourself. Our Buddhist practice helps us examine our lives, to be frank and honest about our true values and beliefs. Our practice of the Lotus Sutra teaches us that honmatsu ku kyo to – constancy from beginning to end – is a truth we learn in Chapter II when we recite the Ten Suchnesses.

Distinction Among Diseases

The doctor helps you with part of this by recommending a specialist for say lungs, or heart, or orthopedic problems. Your doctor recognizes that your issue is beyond his skill and knows who best to treat your condition.

An example of this happened to me recently with some pain in my back and shoulder. My unskilled diagnosis was that I had some muscles in my back pinching a nerve when in fact it turns out that the cause is from arthritis in my cervical column. The doctor suspected as much and sent me to have x-rays taken. Those x-rays revealed significant arthritis. Since I originally wrote this I have had numerous tests and treatments and medications prescribed. I've undergone a couple of months of physical therapy and received a special TENS type device that is much stronger and better than anything over the counter.

There has been significant improvement though still the pain continues. Next up will be injections in the cervical spine to try to shrink the arthritis.

As I have been working through this I have also had a cornea transplant in the right eye and the left eye scheduled in a couple of months. I am optimistic that all of this will greatly alleviate some of the limitations I have been experiencing.

In response to my unskilled diagnosis, I had been applying a heating pad to my back and using my TENS (Trans-cutaneous Electrical Nerve Stimulation) unit on my back without any relief. In fact, the pain extended down my entire right arm, causing me to lose strength in that arm and sensation in my fingers. Now I know I should have been applying heat and the TENS to my neck. I would not have known this without the skill of my doctor.

This is one example of distinction among disease.

Chih-i says: "If you do not know about diseases and yet practice the methods of healing without restraint, since the actions do not match the purpose, there will be no benefit in this."[2]

Here I was, in my ignorance, trying to cure something yet not doing the most beneficial thing to effect such a cure. In fact, I need more skill than I possess, such as physical therapy and perhaps cortisone

---

2   Sweanson, page 1349

shots, though I'm not keen on shots and will need to weigh the risk and the benefits and compare the effects from physical therapy and other less invasive options.

Besides the various illnesses of the body, there are illnesses of the mind. In this, too, it is important to seek out qualified professionals. In the past, I have been approached to provide prayers for mental health issues. I firmly believe that prayers alone will not cure mental illnesses. There have been some who have refused this advice and still expected me to offer prayers or rituals to overcome the illness. Whether we call our mental illness demons, or devils, or traumas, or any name we may wish, they still need to be treated by people who have specialized training in such areas. I do not have that training. I will not mislead anyone or allow anyone to corner me into practicing or providing cure or relief for which I know I am incapable of actuating.

There are special rituals that some Nichiren Shu priests provide, and they can be helpful. I don't discourage anyone from taking advantage of this option when available. The efficacy of such rituals, though, is gained when used to address the spiritual aspect and combined with the medical aspect. Call me what you will, I know too well the dangers of false beliefs, of harmful religious ideations.

Our Buddhist practice is a tool, one tool in a tool box. Medical professionals have additional tools that we lack. Perhaps at some point Nichiren Shu will have priests who are trained therapists or psychologists. But we are not at that point, and so we must combine resources using both faith and practice as well as medical science.

Chanting alone is no sure cure for any illness, except for curing ignorance of the truth of life. We can't chant our way out of dying. To believe so is inconsistent with Buddhism and the many examples in the Lotus Sutra of various Bodhisattvas and personages who go through multiple births and deaths.

We have at our disposal a great truth and the proper way to use it is to apply it to the things for which it is meant to be applied. Chih-i himself was not a doctor, though he compiled and collected all of the current medical wisdom and practice of his time. In his section on contemplation of disease he puts the two side by side, utilizing the specialties of medical wisdom of his time in relation to the Lotus Sutra. If we abandon this approach, then we are not following the wisdom of one of the great minds and practitioners of our lineage.

Faith is the cure to ignorance and the delusion of permanence and independent causation. Faith reveals to us the truth that life progresses to death, that nothing remains unchanged, and that nothing arises without cause.

Our best option is to apply Buddhism to the areas of life for which it is intended and to couple that with the best practices of current medical understanding and treatments. This is an important distinction.

Means

I'm not sure how many of those who read this are familiar with musical instruments. I hope you can at least understand the comparisons I'll make when explaining the sixth of the 10 Characteristics, Means.

Under the section that discusses Means, Chih-i advises that you should skillfully employ healing methods as appropriate. I take this to include the use of doctors and medicines that may be prescribed for your treatment and care. Here I am going to reveal my prejudice to the use of Western medicine.

What informs my preference toward Western medicine would be a fair question to ask. Mainly it boils down to the simple matter of standards and accreditation. I've witnessed instances of practitioners who have no verifiable, no traceable, no standard methods of learning. I'm not saying that all medicine that doesn't come from a MD is bad. I am saying that standards for training may be irregular and potentially incomplete. I am not saying there is no room for improvement in Western medicine or that all MDs are perfect. But at least there is a standard that has a reasonable chance of ensuring that you get competent medical care.

The hospitals I worked with in Charlotte all used what we termed Complementary Care, which included such things as energy healing techniques, massage therapy, aroma therapy, music therapy, and pet therapy, to name a few. In each of these there were licenses and training standards that had to be met and certification before anyone could provide such care. Even the dogs had to have standardized training and certifications.

Some people have asked me about energy healing, which I am trained to do up to Level II in Healing Touch. They have asked me about Reiki, and my response mirrors that of the hospital: Rciki is not generally subject to a standard training curriculum. You don't know who trained your provider and your provider's training and hence their training may not be the same as every other Reiki provider. That may not be a bad thing, but there is no reasonable certainty it is a good thing.

Healing Touch, the program I took, has a standard international training program. Every student undergoes the same training and the trainers are all certified by the same agency to teach the same curriculum. It's the standards and supervision that are critical to me.

Now that is my view. You may have your own. Understand though, when you seek care from non-certified and non-standard sources you are ultimately responsible for the care you receive due to the choices you made. Choose carefully and choose wisely if you decide that Western medicine is not your path.

Choosing which resource to use is yours to make. Choose wisely and skillfully. This applies even to Western medical practices. Remember, you are responsible for your decisions, and it is then up to you to follow the advice given. And not all health care prescriptions are cross compatible, this goes back to Constancy.

Through your Buddhist practice, you can supplement your medical care with other practices. Breath meditation can be useful. Not everyone would be advised to engage in this, especially if you have respiratory issues.

The same goes for chanting. Perhaps you can physically sit and chant; perhaps not. Sitting may be uncomfortable, even laying and chanting may be painful. Recently I was asked by a practitioner what they could do when chanting is so painful that the pain overrides their ability to immerse themselves in the Odaimoku.

What is important to remember in such situations is that your life is also your Odaimoku. The Odaimoku you hold in your mind, even if it is only one every day, is not to be taken lightly. Also, your accumulated practice of your lifetime, even if it is only one day before you became incapacitated, even if only one minute before you were unable to chant, is a profound practice and full of merit.

Cultivating a profound sense of gratitude for even one syllable of the Odaimoku is full of limitless benefit and assures you of enlightenment. If there is one consistent message in the Lotus Sutra it is gratitude and faith.

Chant when you are able. Enjoy that Odaimoku, whether it is said aloud or only in your mind. Hold it. Savor it. Cherish it. Think of it as the finest food you have ever eaten. Would you rush through even a single bite of a rare delicacy? Most likely you would take your time savoring every morsel until it is one and then you would cherish the memory of the taste. If you rushed through the eating, you would miss the taste and have a shallow memory left over.

One Odaimoku is all it takes if done with joy, gratitude, sincerity, and faith. That's the formula for one Odaimoku. Sometimes when we focus on chanting a lot of Odaimoku it is as if we are insecure, feeling perhaps one isn't enough, and so we focus on quantity rather than quality. It is better to chant quality Odaimoku than an abundance of half-quality Odaimoku.

Some may come from Nichiren denominations that have stressed accumulating hours or specific numbers of Odaimoku chanted. While that may not be terrible, I think a more healthy and liberating approach is to know how to chant Odaimoku that fills you up. Learn to chant so that your life fills with quality Odaimoku.

There is a story about a famous Jewish mystic who went from Jewish temple to temple in search of those who pray. At one temple, he opened the door and then left. The usher at the door went after him and asked why he did not come in. His response was that the temple was overflowing with prayer, people's prayer falling off their lips and falling on the floor. There was no room for him to enter. Let us not chant Odaimoku that simply falls off our lips and falls on the floor. Let us chant Odaimoku that ascends to Mt. Sumeru and on to Mount Sacred Eagle.

Now for the comparison to musical instruments that Chih-i employs. Think of any stringed instrument. Chih-i uses a harp. Picture the strings on the instrument of your choice. I play guitar so that is the image I am holding. When you play a musical instrument, there are special techniques that will yield the most pleasing sound. Foremost for stringed instruments is the tuning. This means either tightening or loosening the strings. I also play flute, and this means slight adjustments to the tuning knob near the mouth hole. Tighten either too much and you will be sharp, too loose and you will be flat.

But it isn't only about the instrument outside yourself. It isn't only about the device to make music from. The musician also must consider his or her self as an instrument of either mechanical action on strings or providing wind. The physical instrument is only one aspect to the complete instrument of player and object being played.

The same with our body and illness. There are many factors which our body as the instrument can be influenced by or played by. If we force too much wind then the sound becomes too harsh, or airy. If we pluck the strings too harshly the sound is distorted. If we don't follow the regimen prescribed it is as if a musician didn't practice and so will not be able to attain proficiency. If we treat our healthcare poorly it is as if we tossed our instrument into the corner and didn't clean it or protect it. There are many things to making good music and there are many things that go into living in and through illness.

Time

When a person is ill, time is measured differently than when healthy. In some instances, especially when pain is present, time can seem as if it stands still or even goes backward. Time, Chih-i advises, should not be considered a factor when we are living through illness. He encourages us to focus not on the duration of the illness but on utilization of the methods he outlines and which I am relating to you here.

He doesn't say so specifically, but consider this yourself: If your mind wanders into the realm of time, this is an area where doubt can take root. Doubt can lead to the abandonment of following through on the treatments, both those of medical professionals and of Buddhist practice.

If one does not quickly root our doubts once they arise, addressing the cause of the doubt as well as the nature of the doubt, then they become fertile ground for the arising of even greater doubt. Eventually one may completely abandon one's practice, or one's treatment, or even both. As tempting as it is when one is ill, that is no time to quit your practice, no matter what form it needs to take on. It needs to be firmly held, even built upon.

Indirectly related to this subject, it occurred to me while I was walking my dog, as many ideas do, that we put more effort sometimes and certainly more money frequently into cosmetics and appearance than we do into healthcare and faith.

Once at the hospital there was a woman who needed to have her foot amputated. She had diabetes and a small wound had become incurably infected. She was so afraid of losing her foot. As they rolled her bed out of her room to take her to the surgery area, she was yelling and screaming and crying. I happened to be near her, and I went to her and held her hand the entire trip. There was nothing I could say with my mouth, but I could say with my body that I was present with her. I stayed with her the entire time until they took her into the surgery area.

The nurses told me later that in her room she was fastidious about her hair and her facial makeup. They said when she came in the first time her feet were in really bad condition, her nails were untrimmed, and she had allowed the small sore to become larger. They said she was more concerned with the condition of her exposed body, her face and hair, than she was about the parts that could not be seen.

Foot issues are common in people who have diabetes. There is poor circulation of blood to the feet, which impacts the healing of even the smallest of wounds. If you have diabetes, you should pay particular attention to your feet, something that perhaps many of us aren't always so good at.

Americans spend huge amounts of time and money on cosmetics, not just women, men too. The cosmetics industry is a huge, money-making operation, as well as clothing. That is one of the driving factors behind the increase in men's cosmetic products. We will do, and pay, almost anything to look younger or fight off the appearance of aging. Yet when it comes to the care of our spirit, we don't always give it equal treatment. Of the two the spirit outlasts anything to do with our appearance.

I realize that some care must be given to our skin and hair, and even our wardrobe. Still I wonder how much of that money is spent toward futile endeavors when supporting one's Sangha or community of faith would help not only one's self but would greatly benefit others. Or even if half the money spent on cosmetics, lotions and potions, were donated to the homeless or the hungry, how much our society would improve for many more people.

The point here is to consider the effort and resources spent on appearances compared with care of one's body. I'm not sure we always focus on the most important things. Consider this when you are tempted to call it quits as you live through your illness: It may take a lot of effort but how freely the effort is made to appearances and sometimes begrudgingly to health.

Youth and beauty will vanish. Illnesses will come. Count on it. When getting older and becoming ill, take an equal amount of diligence toward your treatment as you do in your appearance. Of course, there is no need to completely let one's self go. Your looks can be a morale booster. But give equal attention to both treatment and appearance in their measure and requirement.

Selecting and Rejecting

Number seven in the listing of Ten Characteristics given by Chih-i is straightforward in that what works should be continued and what doesn't work should be discontinued. The caveat here is that you must know clearly what is working and what isn't.

Keeping a medical journal or a treatment journal is a necessity, especially if you are living through a long-term illness. The journal can help you keep your pain and treatment in perspective. It gives you a clear record of what is going on. The mind is not a reliable in remembering our health history. The mind is affected by our health. If the mind is being acted upon by pain, then it is not a reliable tool to measure pain, either in absence or in presence.

It is much more reliable to have a clear written record of what you experienced and when. The journal can also serve as a diagnostic aid in your treatment. In this time of ever-shorter doctor-patient office visits, being able to succinctly state when you felt pain, what level it was, how many days it lasted, what areas of the body it occurred on, what you were doing before it began, what you did when it began, what you did when it stopped, if it stopped. There are so many more items that you will not possibly remember after only two weeks, much less a month.

This journal should also include a record of your practice activities. A vague recollection is more harmful sometimes than a clear record. The mind is going to focus on pain and discomfort. That's what our brain is for, to warn us of danger. Three days of pain may seem like no time at all or it may seem like eternity. Yet three days is from either perspective still three days. And the weight of the three days is greater or lesser only in relation to the time surrounding the three days and the limitations on your activities during those three days. You may find from writing that the three days occurred before 5 days of no pain followed by 1 day of pain followed by more pain-free time. You can weigh this, and you can measure this. A vague memory of a lot of pain is not nearly as valuable to you or your healthcare provider.

Also, knowing that you were able to chant 30 minutes in the morning along with a good period of sutra recitation is valuable if you are discouraged because you couldn't do the same in the evening. Perhaps putting more focus on practicing in the morning may yield a greater level of faith time and you can be at peace with doing nothing but attending to your pain in the evening. It is easier to express gratitude if you know where good things happen.

There have been days when 30 minutes of Odaimoku would be cause for great celebration rather than regret or disappointment. Our mind though is more likely to remember what we were unable to do rather than what was successfully accomplished. It is hard to celebrate what you have forgotten, so take the time to record your journey.

Also, recording your journey through illness can provide you with a clear measurable indicator of what is working and what isn't. Simply saying "I don't think this is working" or "I don't feel better" does not give your doctor or your faith adviser much to work on. If however you can say, "When I do this", or "after taking this medicine I felt", or "when I chant I get tired after however many minutes", or "I can't chant in the morning but I can at mid-day", now those are things your partner, whether doctor or faith adviser, can work with.

Your doctors depend on you as much, if not more, than you depend on them. The same goes for your faith companion. Neither can read your mind, nor do they know your body or spirit. When they give instructions or change directions you can record those and compare them to your previous plan to see which is working better for you. Again, this not only helps you, but it is invaluable to your treatment providers.

Protecting

By protecting Chih-i means it is incumbent upon you or your caregiver or both to have a clear understanding and knowledge of any and all restrictions or prohibitions concerning every aspect of your medical care. While this may be challenging to accomplish, it isn't impossible. Here is where you need to stand up and advocate for your own interests.

It isn't that doctors and hospitals don't want to tell you about your condition. It is that they generally only provide basic information, which may or may not cover your unique circumstances.

Things to consider for a treatment plan are: What foods may interact with your medication or recovery, limitations on your physical activities, and the effects of one medication on another. This last concern occurs more often due to compartmentalization of medical care. Taking some medications with others can cause counterproductive results or sometimes even harmful effects. You should always have available the complete listing of your medications and over-the-counter curatives, including vitamins and supplements. This is important to your health. Even if all you do is have a photo on your phone of each of your mediations, it can potentially save your life. This is another reason why it is good, when possible, to get all your medications from the same pharmacy or pharmacy chain.

Do you exercise regularly, walk, or swim, or do yoga or dance? Your doctor won't be able to warn you about restrictions on your exercise if he doesn't know about it. It is also necessary to own up to activities you might not be proud of such as smoking or frequent alcohol or recreational drug use. Don't be ashamed, because your shame may have medical consequences. This is your health, and it is important.

Finally, as boring or tedious as it may seem, it is important to read the information data sheets that accompany your medications. Read with an awareness that what you are looking for is not the worst thing that could possibly happen but information to alert you to potential negative consequences. Also, and this is critically important, always review your dosing instructions. Sometimes a medication can undergo a reformulation that might affect your dose or frequency. You may not be told about it, though hopefully you will be.

Protect your best interest by actively participating in your wellness. Ask questions. Ask, ask, ask. Don't be ashamed or afraid. Don't let anyone's attitude prevent you from acting in your best interest. And it is always in your best interest to ask questions until you understand fully what you should and should not do and what you should expect as normal or abnormal. I have witnessed discharge instructions that differ from verbal to written. Ask for clarification immediately and take notes. Most likely you will forget, or it may become fuzzy after a short while. This is your health and recovery, and it's important.

Know the obstacles.

Here Chih-i says:

> "If you find something effective, do not brag about it publicly, and if you find something ineffective, do not slander or cast doubt on it. In discussing these things with other people, [admit that at times illnesses] that have not yet come to an end or may not come to an end; those that seem to have come to an end may reappear; those that seem to be healed may not have ended; and bringing them to an end again may require the redoubling of effort."[3]

I hope I won't get into too much trouble for this quote. I think this is important to consider. I know how liberating it can feel to proclaim

---

3   ibid, page 1349

X number of years of being cancer-free or declaring having defeated cancer. I get it. And I don't want to be a party pooper. Yet the reality is there is no guarantee that cancer will never re-emerge. I encourage the celebration of overcoming cancer or of being cancer-free, and I encourage the awareness of the feeling of defeat if it recurs. This is the challenge. How do we celebrate health and at the same time know that our health is tenuous and that, in the end, we shall die?

Every day we live is a fact worthy of celebration, with or without cancer. No day is guaranteed to any of us, and that is worthy of celebrating as well. Do not be discouraged by illness, old age, or death. They are not our enemies if we recognize that our natural state is tending toward death from the moment of birth. And while illness and aging are our companions, we need not ignore things we can do to minimize and mitigate their effects on our lives.

Chih-i closes with a statement guaranteeing that if you do these things and have no doubt, it will not be in vain. Based upon my own experience and witnessing others' illnesses and death and the working situation in hospitals, I do believe that following these ten things are worthwhile as a foundation for good self-care and the best insurance you can have for successfully living through and with illness.

13

Cessation

Clarification of Cessation-and-Contemplation

It is reasonable that a person may question how a practice of a religion that fundamentally does not believe in an external solution to the sufferings of life, how that religion could provide a source for support for living with illness. In other words if we don't pray to someone or something to assist us in our suffering then what is it we can accomplish through our Buddhist practice. Since our experience of traditional medicine even going back to Chih-i and beyond it is one of seeking assistance from a source outside of one's self and possibly ingesting or using a substance from outside one's body into or onto one's body. I go to the doctor who is outside of me, and I take a prescription from outside of me and ingest it into my body thus the outside object then affects a curative on the inside of my body.

Buddhism at its fundamental level teaches the Four Noble Truths, the Eightfold Path, and the Twelve Link Chain of Causation and all of those focus on regulating self, body, mind and action. The perspective in Buddhism is from one's self to the outside and medicine is from the outside to the inside. Of course that is a rather simplistic illustration but it is not too inaccurate to the dynamics of self-care, healing, and living through illness. The greatest potential for a breakdown in this harmonious approach is when one favors or excludes on of these elements.

Buddhism is from the inside out and medicine is from the outside in. There is balance and harmony to be achieved to correct the imbalance or disharmony that is occurring in our body, mind, spirit, experience and so forth. Medicine is incapable, at least at this point of curing all disease whether mental or physical. The reason this is true is because of its infancy in understanding the nature of body, mind, and spirit including death and birth. Also in a way medicine hinders itself because it looks at only body or only the brain and rarely at the unity of the two and even less frequently does it even factor in spiritual self.

Buddhism has attempted to consider and teach the principal that there is not separate self from environment or environment from self, no separate mind from body or body from mind, no separate cause from effect or effect from cause. Medicine primarily operates in the cause and effect realm and only recently have begun operating from body and mind and self and environment. The most unexplored area of medicine is the nature of belief and Buddhism has been aware of and instructed in this for thousands of years.

This is why it is important to ensure that one is firmly residing in the practice and teachings of Buddhism as one undergoes medical care and treatment and lives through illness. If we abandon our Buddhist practice and faith then we have cut ourselves off from the healing from self that medicine is incapable of prescribing.

When I worked as a Chaplain in the hospital doing chaplain visits I frequently experience generally two types of response from doctors. One was that the doctors didn't consider the role or function of chaplain as very significant, and only as an afterthought would request a chaplain. Nurses were less prone to this probably because they were closer to the 'front line' and witnessed the benefit to the patient from chaplain support. Some doctors, and this number is increasing, respected, requested, and supported chaplain visits as important to the healing of the patient.

Some doctors were not aware of the level of training a chaplain undergoes to become a certified chaplain. While I don't want to diminish the training a doctor goes through I will say that a chaplain is perhaps the second most trained and skilled provider in a hospital.

Besides the training one goes through in order to be ordained as a minister or priest, there is the additional training of Graduate Level university courses leading to a Masters degree in some theological or divinity degree. Then after that there is the roughly four additional years of Chaplain training including over 3000 hours of clinical experience. Finally before certification one must undergo a review board examination as well as examination of writing amounting to roughly an inch thick of paper (mine was a little over one inch, single sided, 10pt type, one inch margins, lol how well I remember those guidelines). This is more training than a nurse undergoes. I say all of this knowing that there is no way I could qualify to be a nurse or doctor and I would fail miserably at memorizing all the things they need to recall. Yet we each have our specialty and we each train with our hearts and minds and bodies to accomplish our passion and goal.

What one believes is what one experiences. Also often times people do not know what they believe. Further complicating this is the hidden beliefs a person has accumulated from various experiences and the effect of those hidden beliefs on our health.

When I first began working with boys dying of AIDS, the diagnosis meant a death sentence. The same used to be the case with Cancer. Now HIV/AIDS is treatable and there has been some examples cure and reversal. The same has been the case for Cancer. But the advances in medicine are not often identical to the beliefs of individuals or society. HIV/AIDS still caries a stigma of death and contagion in many parts of society and the world, yet this notion is contrary to the science. Many times when a person is diagnosed with Cancer the immediate mental gymnastics does a pole vault right to death. Yet there are so many types of Cancer and so many cures.

The hidden messages from society are when someone learns a friend has cancer the most common reaction, and I am taking this from what I have witnessed and personally experienced is "Oh my gosh you're going to die" even if those are not the words spoken it is the undertone of the expressions. They may not be the words but it is clearly obvious in the way people act. And sometimes it is even "you're going to die tomorrow" which is absurd except for some rare and aggressive types of cancer.

This makes it extremely challenging for even the most positive minded person to maintain a positive mindset. This can be one of the reasons why people don't share their trajectory through illness. It gets tiring trying to maintain a positive mindset when everyone else exhibits fear of you dying and dying soon. It also get tiring hanging the emotions of others when your own emotions are requiring so much work to stay focused on your own mental and physical health.

Then there is the opposite extreme where people stop asking or seeming to not care because they don't want to upset the person who is ill. They sometimes feel like if they asked it would be like picking a scab on a wound. Or they may not connect because they are unsure what they can do or should do.

My best advice, though not the easiest, is talk about what you're feeling. Understand though that the feelings of the person with the illness trumps all other feeling of others. Also rather than leaving it out there as "let me know if there is anything I can do" actually offer to do something. Perhaps you might say, would you object to me bringing some casserole that I am baking on Friday? I can drop off a couple of servings and it will be no trouble to do so?" In other words make a concrete offering. Rather than putting the burden on the sick person try being proactive in suggesting something. "Can I bring you some flowers for decoration, I'll be out shopping on Tuesday and it would not a be problem?" If refused accept the refusal not as an affront or a refusal of any support just understand that right now there is no need. It isn't that the person hates you or doesn't appreciate your offering.

"Would you like for me to pick any groceries while I am shopping next Wednesday?" Perhaps the answer will be no this week but yes the next time. If you can do something and are willing to do it, then offer it and understand that perhaps this time might not be best but next time might be perfect. If however your offering of support is conditional to them praising you or being in debt to you then it really is best to refrain from helping until you can do so freely.

It is sort of like Dhana. True Dhana is offering and support given without any expectation of reward or benefit.

When a child is born it is not normal that we say "Oh, the poor thing is going to die", we don't say to the parents, "I am so sorry for the eventual death of your child." Instead we naturally celebrate the life and birth of the child, even though those two previous statements are completely accurate and honest.

What I am talking about is balance in all situations in life. A balance between life and death, between optimism and pessimism. The Buddha abandoned his austerity practice and his search for the perfect intellectual teaching and sat under the Bodhi tree and attained an enlightenment of the Middle Way between denial and abundance and intellect only.

I will borrow from a story that can perhaps illustrate this. One time there was a skilled mountain climber who decided one morning before the sun rose to scale the side of a familiar mountain. After about half way up his ascent a piece of the side of the mountain which he had placed his shifting weight upon broke off. Suddenly he began to fall. Fortunately there was a root which he was able to grab hold of. After a few minutes though the root began to peel away fro the mountain side and our climber found himself dangling from this root a thousand feet from the rocks below and as the vine or root swung out he was 15 or 20 feet from the side of the mountain.

As he gripped the root ever more tightly he knew his time to hold on was decreasing due to the strain. As he began to settle his mind into the situation he found that he didn't need to grip so tightly and could hold on longer. Looking up he noticed a berry, perhaps a strawberry or a grape. It was within his reach and so he grabbed it. With his free hand he popped it into his mouth and savored the juices and the sweetness of the fruit. Wow he thinks to himself this is the sweetest most delicious fruit he had ever tasted. Never before had he eaten a fruit so slowly and took the time to taste it in such a way. The pending fall to the rocks below, the certainty of his death allowed him to notice a richness of the experience heretofore unnoticed.

Just at this moment the sun begins to peak above the surrounding mountains and he declares this to be the most beautiful dramatic sunrise he had ever seen.[1]

Resist the urge at this point to read further. Take a moment to taste the experience with your life. Resist the urge to know what happens.

Death is death, life is life. It is our choice as to how we will experience them both.

Buddhism teaches us the way to master our mind to ward off evil and to strengthen the resources within ourselves to accomplish our indestructible joy, how to become enlightened. By perfecting our minds through our practice of meditation, chanting the Odaimoku, reciting the sutra and study of Buddhist principles we can buttress up the fortress of our mind thereby ensuring that the misfortunes that fall upon our body is incapable of shaking our faith.

----

1   Mitchell Chefitz, 2002, The Seventh Telling: The Kabbalah of Moeshe Kapan, St. Martins Press, story credit

Chih-i says that even if a huge mountain like obstacle arises if we have perfected our practice and continue to strengthen our faith and practice then you can be able to face even death and sacrifice your remaining breaths to remaining in what he calls the 'meditation chamber'. He assures that there is no offense or karma that can not be overturned or extinguished. We can find this in the words of the Lotus Sutra, and we can take great comfort in them.

Chih-i's approach is to view conventional reality as not an illusion to be denied but a positive interpretation of the meaning of emptiness. So in the reality of our life the goal is not to deny what we experience. Rather the objective is to see the reality of the emptiness of those experiences and that reality, is the basis of the Middle Path.

We do not deny the pain we may experience, instead we embrace the positive aspect of that pain as an indicator that there is a way between completely succumbing to the inevitability of pain and the denial of pain. The pain in a way is the reality which we can use to experience life and move between surrender and ignorance.

There is a balance that is possible that stabilizes the mind, spirit, and body. Buddhism is the tool to do this most effectively because it does not deny or celebrate but teaches an honest awareness of the true nature of reality. There is birth, there is life, there is sickness, there is disease, there is death.

Perhaps another story? There is an anti-racist tale attributed to the Buddha about a yaksa demon. This particular fellow was ugly with a capital U and he had an evil color. What color would we say that is, what would be an evil color to you? Well needless to say he wasn't too welcome by everyone. They didn't like his looks. Folks became angry when he showed up.

The 'Thirty-Three Devas' became so agitated that they went to Indra saying the demon must be removed. Indra then with respect and with great politeness approached the demon who then willing agreed to not appear anymore. The Buddha or Indra, depending on how and who tells this, used this story to scold the 'Thirty-Three Devas' and teach about the danger of harboring anger, hatred, and ill-will and judging (particularly on the basis of color).[2]

When we experience something unpleasant in out lives, pain perhaps, we can easily become tense and resentful of the pain. I know I need to constantly remind myself to be gentle on my physical imitations while at the same time avoiding become complacent with these new limits. If I approach my limits with kindness and appreciation them for what they can teach me while at the same time not avoiding them, not hating them, and not being too nice to them then I am more at peace. When I can do this I find that I'm actually able to do a little bit more than perhaps I thought I could. Now that may not be everyone's experience. Certainly though making an enemy of our pain, usually does not make it go away any faster and may even provide fertile ground for that demon to grow uglier, large, and more colorful.

Chih-i reminds us that when the lord of the castle is determined and hard as a rock, the guards are also strong. When the lord is timid, then the guards will be busy, distracted, and possibly hasten to run away. You are the lord and the castle is your body. The guards are the two gods of the same name and same birth as yourself. When you are born it is said that there are two protective guardians who appear at the moment of birth with your same birth time and your same name. They reside with you your entire life and watch over you your entire life. Their strength is given to them by your actions and beliefs. These are the guards who protect your castle according to their lord. "If your mind is firm, then you are strong; the same is true for the body and its guardian deities."[3]

The teaching of Clarification of Cessation-and-Contemplation is broken down into ten sections. As I did on the Ten Characteristics I'll present the ten sections with some further explanation. For this section there is actually in some cases not a clear distinction from

---

2   Swanson, page 1350

3   Swanson, page 1351

one to the next, the transition is subtle. I will rely upon the general division presented by the translator Paul Swanson, though these divisions do not necessarily occur in Chih-i's writing.

The main emphasis of these ten sections is on contemplating objects as inconceivable, it is by far the longest entry in this section and a few are only a sentence or several words long. Let us begin.

Slightly out of sequence I will offer a story hopefully one to encourage you in your effort of developing a resolute mind and attitude to your Buddhist practice and faith as you live through disease. It is a story which some folks in the US, perhaps especially from the Southern States may recognize though there is no proof the US version arose from the Buddhist version.

This is the story of Stuck to a Demon in Five Places. In a former lifetime of the Buddha he was once a chief merchant at the head of a group of merchants. One day he and his party were traveling through a difficult mountainous regions and came across a demon who obstructed his passage. The demon shouted "Stop! Do not move! I will not allow you passage!" Something like "you shall not pass!" from Lord of the Rings except in this case it is the bad guy saying it.

Scoffing at the demon the chief merchant saunters up and strikes him with his right fist, unfortunately for the merchant his fist stuck to the demon. So the merchant rears back and with his left fist he strikes the demon and the left fist remains glued to the demon. Next he kicks with his right foot, and it too remained stuck. Following the right foot the merchant kicks out with is left foot, which also remains glued to the demon. The demon laughs at him and merchant gives him a head butt, and now his head is glued to the demon. Continuing his demonic laugh the demon taunts him further and says, "Now what are you going to do? Do you give up?"

The merchant replies that even though five parts of his body remain immobile due to adhering to the demon his mind remains unfettered, his mind remains resolute in not giving up and not giving in to the demon. The merchant says that he will continue to fight the demon with all of his mind. The demon is impressed with the determination and strength of mind the chief merchant has and so agrees that his mind is very strong and he deserves to be able to pass.

While various parts of our body may become 'glued' to the demon of our illness it is crucial that our mind remains determined and focused on not giving up. Our body may be defeated but our mind is stronger than any of our organs or limbs. It is important to treasure this and nourish our mind with our determined Buddhist practice. The best time to begin doing this is before we become ill so that we have developed the path to follow when we may be weakest.

1. Objects as Conceivable and Inconceivable

Conceivable objects are those which can be conceptually understood. The causes and conditions of disease [dis-ease] precipitate the rise of the ten dharma realms or as we frequently refer to them, the Ten Worlds. The Ten Worlds encompass the realms from Hell to Buddha. Because of dis-ease you may tend to retreat from Buddha and loose your pure mind to aspire to enlightenment. There is a serious concern that because of the effects of dis-ease it may affect your willingness to engage in meditation, chanting the Odaimoku, or reciting the sutra. It may even come about that your dis-ease causes you to slander the Three Jewels of Buddhism, the Buddha, the Dharma, and the Sangha.

Especially the mind becomes susceptible to thoughts such as looking and dwelling on past offenses or behaviors. You may begin to blame your past for your present circumstances. Further it may be tempting to say that all of your good and sincere efforts have failed to protect you and that your practice has not benefited you. You may be tempted to say Buddhism has been of not value because now you are dis-eased.

On the reverse side of this is the actions when recovery is accomplished. You may say that you did it on your own and ignore the times in your past before your illness of your practices. You may even say that your faith allowed you to recover and so now you can do anything you wish as if you were immortal.

Disease, Illnesses are not as simple as these thoughts and the temptation to dwell in such simplistic and unhealthy religious ideations is great, a trap waiting for our weakness or our disregard for the truths of the Dharma.

Cultivating a strong mind focused on proper meditation and mindfulness is fundamental and should be a constant endeavor whether in good or poor health.

These are the ways in which disease become a cause for producing the conditions for the three evil realms of Hell, Animality, and Hunger. This is why we should not fall into the traps and take seriously the cautions of avoiding the harmful thoughts above.

If however, you are aware that we are personally responsible for our destiny and that disease does cause suffering brought about by a lack of good deeds in the past and then are truly contrite about our behaviors, reflecting upon the nature of our actions in the past and without recrimination determine to change our patterns of behavior even in the face of the disease we can then transform the sufferings of disease into the cause for producing the three god destinies of pretas, humans, and divine beings.

When I give instructions prior to performing the Hokke Senbo ceremony, the ceremony traditionally translated as repentance, I expand upon the translated title. I teach that it is not enough to say only repentance. In fact we should reflect upon our behavior, our actions and our thoughts. It is necessary to do this so that we can in clear light examine the nature of our cause, the cause for the cause and understand how we might respond differently in the future if the same opportunity were to happen again. Further it is not enough to repent and reflect because that in a way leave a vacuum and it lacks and action to fill the void made by repenting and reflecting. Once we repent and then reflect I believe it is further necessary to makes some action to ensure a different result in the future.

This is not simply doing a good deed, although it never hurts to engage in abundantly doing good deeds. Rather is what sort of deed will begin to altar the pattern of behavior. Karma is after all an action word, it is the action we take in response to an affect we experience. Our present is the accumulation of all of our past actions, our karma. To change our karma begins by acting differently in the present. So from the effort of repenting and reflecting what new pattern of behavior will emerge.

If we think of repenting and reflecting as tearing down the rough and bumpy road of our life we must also think about creation. What new road of life will we create? This is how disease can be a cause for elevating one's life from the three lower evil realms.

If becoming ill, encountering disease brings about fear of death or of the cycle of birth and death then it is crucial that you understand fully that birth leads to sickness and death. Avoiding this truth only leads to future lifetimes of continued suffering from sickness and death. Suffering makes you weak and this weakness puts you in peril of forgetting this truth thereby ensuring its continuation. In these moments of thought Chih-i admonishes us to seek the quiet of extinction and nirvana, thus disease becomes the cause for entering the realm of sravakas.

How disease is the cause for Pratyekabuddha is the longest section within this portion of Cessation. Basically it begins with a firm understanding of the Twelve Link Chain of Causation and the awareness that nothing arises independently of anything else. I often think sometimes as Buddhist we focus so much on the Four Noble Truths and the Eightfold Path that we don't emphasize as much the concept of dependent origination as revealed in the Twelve Link Chain. I won't go into the entire theory, primarily because it is easy enough to research it via the internet and even within the Lotus Sutra itself. Basically this teaching informs us that birth comes about because of past existences which have lead to grasping, passion, contact, six senses, name and form of four elements and five sense organs and name refers to the sense organ of mental, leading eventually to ignorance and rebirth.

In this portion of Cessation Chih-i advises us to focus on where our illness arises from, this is not the same as understanding the medical cause of the particular disease, rather it is the complete awareness that life is the condition for disease. It is important to stress this is not simply a mental exercise and theoretical awareness or knowledge alone of the nature of dependent origination is not what is to be sought. The goal is a deep abiding full heart embraced truth awareness. Simply knowing the Twelve Links is not the same and embracing them. I can't stress this enough. Because you can recite the various causes of arising does not indicate a true life awareness or deep heart connection to the fundamental truth. This is why ignorance is said to be the key to breaking the cycle of the Twelve Link Chain. It is not ignorance of the causes from a mental or mind standpoint, it is ignorance of thinking without truly understanding from within ones life.

Knowledge can lead to full understanding but knowledge alone is not itself true understanding. Knowledge helps to break down the logic of the teaching but it is not the same as embracing the teaching as a core life value.

For this section contemplating the various origins of various qualities and parts of our life is the first step it is the tool for beginning to become fully aware. This is how disease can cause pratyekabuddhahood.

Here is one exercise presented in this section. Contemplate that the color blue-green arises from wood. The color yellow arises

from earth, red from fire, white from wind, black from water.
Contemplate them not as the simple series I just typed but as
progressive steps. Contemplate the arising of each color from its
corresponding element.

Next contemplate the arising of wood from water, water from
wind, wind from earth the positive chi energy or the yang, earth
from fire, fire from wood and back again to wood from water.
Once again do not simply contemplate is a the series I abbreviated
but as individual distinct arisings. This cultivates and awareness
of the cycle of arisings, that one leads to another to another and
finally back again to the origin. Nothing arises alone or from itself.

On to the organs from the above external things. The liver arises
from blue-green chi-energy. The heart arises from red-chi energy.
The lungs from white chi-energy. The kidneys arise from black
chi-energy. The spleen from yellow chi-energy.

We know that none of these organs arise from itself independent
of the other organs and life does not arise without all of the organs.
The liver arises from kidneys, which arise from the lungs, which
arises from spleen, which arises from the heart, which arises
from the liver, and we are back again with the awareness that the
liver does not arise from itself but from the kidneys. This is the
understanding and teaching of Chih-i.

If by doing this we and seeking full awareness and understanding
about the nature of internal matters of our body of the four
elements and five organs we can see they are without substantive
essence. There is no essential kidney that arises or exists beyond
its relationship to the other organs. There is no essential element
of wood that exists beyond its relationship to the other elements
of water, wind, and fire. You are not simply a kidney a tree or
wood is not simply wood. Everything exists in relation to and in
connection with other things.

Because there is no essential kidney rather a kidney in relation
with other organs it has no essential substance. Because it has no

essential substance it is indestructible. It is the mind that maintains its essential substance or nature.

The Mind holds the essence or essential nature of each organ the mind can distinguish between the kidney, the heart, the spleen and so forth. In that regard there is no essential substance to destruct and so it is indestructible.

The four mental or four skandas maintain the essence of the four elements and five organs. The mind or skanda of consciousness maintains earth. "The mental skanda of conceptions maintains wind. The mental skanda of sensations maintains fire. The mental skanda of volitions maintains water. Therefore they are indestructible and do not pass away completely."[4]

So next Chih-i asks us to ask ourselves if these minds or skandas arise on their own or do they not? We can surmise based upon the theory of dependent origination that do not independently arise and this would be correct. There is no exception to dependent origination not even in other theories. Buddhism is not illogical even if it may be difficult to comprehend at times.

If I might inject here as you wrestle with these perhaps new concepts that fundamentally the most important take away is to internalize the embrace without doubt or reservation the truth of dependent origination as a truth that is found in all other truths, including the Four Nobel Truths, the Eightfold Path, and of course the Twelve Link Chain of Causation. There is not study of Buddhism that can be considered legitimate if it does not pass the test of no independently arising phenomena. If it appears by magic without a cause then it isn't Buddhism.

Onward onto volitions arise from sensations, sensations arise from conceptions, conceptions arise from consciousness, consciousness arises from volitions from the past, volitions from the past arise from ignorance, ignorance arises from deluded conceptions, and

---

4   Swanson, page 1353

finally deluded conceptions arise from deluded conceptions. No that is not a typo or editorial error.

Deluded conceptions arise from deluded conceptions is the complete turning of the twelve conditions as the sutra says. Suvarnaprabhasa Sutra.[5]

There is a wonderful visual story Chih-i provides to illustrate this point in his own words. Sadly I know that I would be in violation of copyright laws if even attempted to retell it. The story is unique and long and beyond my ability to retell it.

Instead I'll offer what may be a different way of illustrating this. Suppose you are playing a video game. My only experience of playing a video game is from several years ago when I returned to college to get my degree. Most of my classes were comprised of much younger students and since many of them were in the same major as I was we matriculated in many classes together. Over a short period of time and because I was intentional about interacting with the young people and they were perhaps curious about this older person we became good, even close friends. At the time they were all playing World of Warcraft, WoW. Listening to them talk about the experience was intriguing to me so I decided to give it a try.

At first, being new to the whole online game experience I was a total looser. In fact some of them actually took me around almost on a leash getting me gear and completing quests until I got the hang of it. The sheltered me for a while and it helped tremendously. None of that is germain to the story it is merely

---

5   ibid, page 1353

The phrase contained in the above sutra says "The causes and conditions of deluded conceptions merge and come into existence; they do not really exist on their own, but are conveniently named and based upon ignorance."

background information a sort of how it happened and why I know anything about gaming at all even if only a teeny tinny bit.

So, at first the visual of the online game experience is obviously not real. Nothing comes close to being anything like real life, you can tell it is all computer. Now that doesn't mean the figures don't act lifelike. In fact the more I found I allowed my self to be immersed in the game the more the distinction between what was obviously not real and what one would consider real life real became more subtle and in fact would even perhaps vanish. It is a combination of intensity of the experience the emotional investment in the game and accomplishing various things as well as the very human and real interaction through voice and text with other human players who are represented by the various digital characters on the screen.

Now here is the thing, if a person, and I've seen or witnessed this and perhaps to some degree at times I experienced it myself, if a person allows themselves to fully enmesh into the game and the character and the role being played it can become real as real perhaps are real life real. Crazy huh. And yet this is not a rare phenomena. Perhaps some of the readers of the blog have more experience with online games than I do can perhaps attest to this as well.

So when you then transfer your online personality to your physical real life flesh and bones body forgetting that you are not in the game any longer then a deluded conception or thought (the online character) gives rise to deluded conception or thought (the real life character thinking they are the online character) and visa versa. Sadly this isn't as graphic as Chih-i's story though this is a bit more contemporary. Hopefully it makes sense. It's hard to tell sometimes when you write if what you write will be understood by the reader as you intended or even at all.

The point here is that by understanding this by seeking to understand this dependent origination as we live with and through disease can be the cause for our entering the realm of pratyekabuddhahood.

As I have been studying this and thinking deeply on the subject it is easy to see that these very same principles can be applied to any and every aspect of our lives. What condition or realm of the Ten Worlds do our experiences cause to arise? When we navigate our lives what is our perception? What delusions to we suffer from and thus cause the arising of conditions which only ensure continued suffering? Are we able to transform our experiences and use them is wholesome and skillful ways to cause the arising of higher realms which enable us to reduce our suffering and also enable other to begin to eliminate their suffering? I think these are interesting questions which arise from our understanding and contemplation on disease and dis-ease.

So throughout this book we have learned how imbalances have been created in our lives which lead to various experiences of disease. When we focus to heavily on physical body, life, and wealth we create imbalances; any singular focus inherently ignores something. Singular focuses also increase the level of stress due to the constant vigilance on one aspect which over time drains of the energy and resources to focus on the larger picture of the many aspects of wellness.

We too have learned that if our spiritual practice if our attention to mind and spirit have been neglected then we deprive ourselves of the vast resources and healing power of mind and spirit. If we are not able to have calm forbearance, or if our resolution is weak, we leave our spirit unguarded and vulnerable.

Also if we are not diligent in our actions, not only in relation to our health and wellness but also in our actions in society and the environment we subject ourselves to dangers of misfortune. We can not lightly misuse or abuse our environment either large or small, immediate or further beyond, without avoiding the accumulation of a myriad of negative effects. Our causes have effects consequent to them.

Further, if we lack wisdom or have little wisdom and if we fail to penetrate understanding of disease and the transient nature of suffering, emptiness, no-self this leads to further and increased suffering from illness and disease.

If however, your illness causes you to expand your life and have compassion for others who suffer from illness and disease, if you have pity for others in their pain and limitations then disease arouses compassion. The arousal of compassion due to our own awareness of living through and in illness and disease hopefully will lead to making a vow to help others. This compassion helps us see that since all phenomena are insubstantial and transient then for us to abandon our own suffering without regret is made easier. In accord with the principal of attaining calm endurance with no regret and increasing our efforts of correct intentions and awakening. These are the causes of dis-ease that arouse the realm of Tripitaka bodhisattva of the six perfections.

Contemplating dis-ease and becoming aware that disease arises from delusion, perversion, misconceptions, passions and its afflictions, in this life and previous existences helps us to realize and awaken to the reality that both self and nirvana are empty. In this case dis-ease is the cause of the realm of the bodhisattva of the Shared Teachings.

Going even deeper still in our contemplation of dis-ease we find that dis-ease is ultimately empty, that there is no place of self that experiences disease yet all experiences are conventionally experienced. That is when we make our experiences more solid then we become attached to the experience which is a hindrance. Again, understanding that there is not fundamental self that self is an empty concept except, yes there is a physical body, there is a thinking mind but going deeper beyond that there is not self that resides permanently and independently of the entire universe.

I share with you one of my favorite ways of imaging this concept. If you consider a wave on the ocean, you can see the wave arise from the surface of the ocean. There are many factors that cause a wave to arise. Some of those factors are the relationship between the earth and the moon, the geological formations under the surface of the ocean, the temperature of the water and the ever changing circulation of water because of the temperature, winds on the surface also affect and cause waves, then too there are the effects of geological phenomena such as volcanoes or earthquakes. In short there are numerous causes for the arising of waves.

While I am no expert on waves it might be safe to guess that perhaps no two waves are exactly identical, after all the water is constantly circulating and never in the same spot for long. And as someone who has surfed and who swam in the Pacific Ocean in Hawaii I can say that waves have personalities almost, some are favorable for surfing if you catch the right spot, some not so good.

We can look at waves and discern that some waves are different in appearance and also in behavior. Each wave or group of waves has characteristics that may be similar to others around it, sort of like how we group up in society.

But when you examine a wave you see that fundamentally it is only the water of the ocean which has formed in such a way and will only exist for a limited duration of time. At the end of the cycle of life of the wave what is it? It is simple the water of the ocean. The water retains no identifiable marker showing it was a part of wave number six on Sunset Beach Hawaii at six o'clock in the morning on March 8, 1975 and ceased to exist 20 minutes later. The wave existed and then the wave didn't exist. The water continues the wave does not. There is no fundamentally permanently existing wave unique and continuing.

Our lives are similar in many ways. We came into existence because certain conditions were favorable to our live. We live and we travel on the ocean of life as our named wave. Here is the thing though we are not separate from the universe and the essence of life throughout time and space. We have this illusion that I am unique, I am special, I am permanent, I am forever. These attachments are convenient until they cause us suffering; suffering of expectation of perfect happiness, perfect health, longevity, importance, uniqueness, and desire for permanence and eternity as self. The only thing that separates each of us simply our karma, the accumulation of previous causes.

Some people may find this troubling, I understand that. It has taken me a long time to grapple with this to embrace it in peace and to let go of the fear of impermanence. I find it quite liberating. It was not easy and even still it does require maintenance especially when I become attached to memory.

When our experience of dis-ease in disease causes us to extinguish experience and accept enlightenment then it is the case that dis-ease is the cause of the realm of the bodhisattva of Distinct Teachings.

Throughout all of this we can see that it is possible for dis-ease to cause us to gradually step-by-step give rise or elevate our condition of life to higher levels of attainment. This is the conceivable-realm and helps us understand what is not desirable to contemplate.

1. Objects as Inconceivable

I'm not sure many of us have considered illness or disease as inconceivable, especially since we are experiencing it and so we are deluded into thinking it is conceivable (conceptually understood). Yet there is an aspect to disease, dis-ease, that is also, perhaps for a lack of a better way of conceptualizing this, metaphysical in nature. Let's see if I can clarify this.

Currently the Veterans Administration is monitoring my health for two major, potentially serious matters. One is a tumor in my lung which has the appearance of being cancer. The other is a more recent finding that the first vertebrae in my spine, the one directly connected to my skull is fractured. In both of these there is an awareness on the part of the doctors of each problem, there is also an unawareness of the degree of potential harm, the tumor, and the potential solution, the spine and the tumor.

For me, the spine issue is very painful and very debilitating. Also because I have not yet had an MRI on the area of the spine there is a lack of information as to the degree of the fracture and so it is not possible to begin any treatment due to the risk of causing further damage. The tumor in the lung while contributing to diminishment of breathing function is less obvious, especially on a moment by moment basis. Of the two however the most serious one to the longevity of my life is the tumor.

So the least obvious issue is the most threatening and the most painful and constantly obvious issue is the least important to longevity of life. So the issue of the tumor while not really metaphysical medically speaking is experientially almost entirely metaphysical. Does that make sense, I hope so.

Remember earlier in the book I wrote about pain and pain research and how after a period of long term pain, pain becomes its own thing. Pain becomes a real almost separate thing beyond merely a feeling or sensation. Pain becomes an entity in and of itself beyond the thing triggering the pain. Yet the pain is not fundamentally a thing but an experience. The pain transitions from being an experience to a substantive matter. Yet in our experience of the pain, and without the medical technicalities pain has no essence beyond the experience in relation to the thing causing the pain. Pain in that situation while real is sort of metaphysical, at least in our experience.

The lack of pain from the tumor in my lung is also somewhat metaphysical in that there is really pain there, from the sense of disruption of harmony in my lung. By rights since the 'pain' in my lung and the tumor that exists is potentially the most dangerous condition to longevity that pain should be more pronounced.

So to some degree hopefully you can see that there is an inconceivable nature of illness and disease. Another way to think of it, though not philosophically accurate is to consider germs and bacteria. We can't see them unaided and so they are sort of like sneaky inconceivable little gremlins waiting of an opportune moment to attack us. They are not in themselves nefarious it is just that their existence and the environment they need to live in is harmful and not in our human life best interest. Sort of like humans existing in the environment of the earth, we are not necessarily in the best interest in the continuation of a healthy balanced eco-system of the planet. We are a bacteria which is killing our good Mother Nature. This is also perhaps inconceivable, certainly almost intangible.

A single thought moment of disease is not real and does not fundamentally exist but it does exist phenomenally, because all phenomena are involved in dis-ease, and those phenomena do not go beyond that involvement. These phenomena are dis-ease phenomena and while we might find similar looking phenomena in other experiences they are not the 'same' phenomena because of the relation to the unique experience. The phenomena of hell in dis-ease is not distinct from the phenomena of any of the other realms, it is the same phenomena only our understanding of, awareness, utilization, understanding, and actions make the phenomena distinct. There is no unique realm of the phenomena that is hell other than our action in relation to the phenomena. It is beyond our ability to verbally express it is in essence pure, and only our interpretation assigns it as one value over another. In this way the reality of dis-ease is inconceivable. Chih-i says it is like the wish-fulfilling jewel. The jewel is neither empty or full, it simply resides as a potential, and regardless of whether the wish is used for good or ill, the jewel is not the nature of the wish.

Drawing again on my own current condition of the fractured vertebrae. The pain at times is almost unbearable, sometimes I'm unable to sleep, sometimes I simply want to curl in on myself and become as small as possible in the hope that a smaller me will be a smaller surface of pain. I am also unable to hold things at times in my right hand, the muscles simply do not work. Further I have lost feeling in my pinky and ring finger of the right hand. I'm sharing this not for sympathy, simply as a way to provide some illustration to these concepts. Also I'm sharing so that perhaps you can see into some of my ways of understanding beyond mere theory and from a practical application point of view.

Words are cheap, actions are much more expensive.

The loss of grip and feeling means that frequently I am unable to hold a pen to write with. The loss of feeling also means that I can not sense how my hand rests on the writing surface and how much pressure or contact I am making with the writing instrument. The loss of feeling in the two fingers make typing very challenging. I can't tell when I have hit a key with enough pressure to actually cause the key to 'strike'. Typing means I need to look at every character as it appears on the screen and not rely on touch-typing. Typing this manuscript has been challenging because I make so many mis strikes and so many typing errors I am constantly hitting the backspace key to redo what I wrote. It is annoying and frustrating, though I am learning a certain amount of forbearance in the process. Not being able to grip and feel means that holding a knife to carve blocks for printing is to some degree not safe and to another degree certain to yield poorly carved blocks.

These issues in and of themselves are not life threatening with reasonable caution. They certainly are annoying, even discouraging and of course that can lead to a decrease in desire to live which greatly affects longevity. Now, please do not worry, I am not experiencing and decrease in my desire to live. I'm only sharing it to show how the cycle could continue and how it does for many people who live with long term disabilities.

Now all of these symptoms have no fundamental value, they are not hell nor are they Buddha or Bodhisattva. They are empty, even if annoying in their limitations. The key is what do I do, how do I react, how do I live in the pain and limitations, not just how do I live with. To me living in is slightly different than living with. I live with the tumor in my lung, it is there, unwelcome, and does not greatly affect my day to day living; of course that may change.

I can choose to live with my pain, meaning that my life is always less than it was due to the pain and limitations. I can also try to choose to live in the pain or live through the pain by learning a new way of living that brings me joy even if the means is different. So, I can't carve right now, that may or may not become permanent. In the mean time what other things can I do that will bring me joy? Well building Legos models is one thing, doing collage and some painting is also possible and joyful. I can still walk and play with my dog. So life in pain will perhaps look different than it did before pain. The pain is not the limitation when I live in pain, I am the limitation or the expansion of joy and activity in pain. I think here the English language is failing us. Living in pain is not to me the same as being in pain, or a painful existence. I live in Syracuse NY, I live in a two story house, I live many things, and I live in pain. It snows there a lot during winter, the snow sometimes limits my outdoor activities, there is pain in my body and sometimes that limits my activities.

I am not dispassionate about my pain. My doctor and physical therapists can tell you I am not for sure as I have sometimes in weak moments let my frustration slip out in my language and interactions. I think that is human, or perhaps I want to give myself an excuse to be weak. I care about my pain and how much it hurts at times, but the pain is not the enemy or at least not one powerful enough to control my entire life. Living in pain means that it is there, it is part of my sensory experiences, it has affects on my body, and it is not evil or good it simply is. It is the degree I allow it to control my joy, my experiences of life, my desire to live which is under my control. The pain is not in charge, unless I give in to it.

The pain is in a way a wish-fulfilling jewel, it sits there hanging out on my nerve endings doing its thing like its supposed to do

warning me of damage someplace in my body, and it sits there
doing what it is designed to do and waits for me to decide how I
will use it, what wish will I make and act upon.

This pain, and my illnesses are in a way tentative diseases like
what I discussed earlier in the book, they perhaps exist as tools
to allow me to teach. What do you think? I think it depends on
me what use or value I put on them. They can be Mara, if I allow
myself to be defeated, even if limited and debilitated, or they can
be Golden Buddhas inspiring me to do the necessary work of
teaching the Lotus Sutra. They have no intrinsic value other than
the value my life gives them.

This way dis-ease, disease, and illnesses are inconceivable objects.

I've brought up pain and I would like to diverge slightly away
from Chih-i for a moment. Over the past several years doctors and
nurses have been asking people to rate their pain on a scale, usually
1-10. Some people are not quite sure about how they are supposed
to rate pain, it hurts and they want it to stop. Some fear if they say
it is too low, then their pain will be ignored. Other don't want to
be thought of as weak and so they fear rating their pain too high.

Here is how I measure my pain. You may find it helpful or you
may not, it's just my way of figuring out how to rate something
that hurts and I want it to stop. If the pain prevents me from
sleeping, doing normal activities, inhibits my doing and engaging
in things that add value to my life then I rate the pain high from
8-10 or so. If the pain makes doing those things difficult but not
impossible then I'll rate my pain at 6-8. If the pain is constant and
causes me to be aware of it frequently to always then I rate the pain
at 6-8. If the pain is an annoyance, bearable and present but not
always thought of then I rate it 4-6. If there is pain and it is off and
on and never debilitating or limiting then I rate it 2-5.

These are not hard and fast ratings, merely a reference point for
where I start looking for numbers to answer their question. I

always briefly in only a few words indicate what I based the measure on. For example the other day when I went to the physical therapy evaluation for my fractured neck vertebrae I said the pain was 9-10 based upon it interrupts and interferes with sleep and prevents me from doing important life fulfilling activities. The nurse nodded her head and said yes, those would be a 10. I shared my range of numbers and what my rating was based upon and then she could fine tune the scale to the degree she needed to record my pain.

Does that make sense to you. I know sometimes it is challenging to communicate with medical providers. Pain is one of those areas. Because we have no effective way to measure pain, see pain, analyze pain the 1-10 scale is an attempt at providing a reasonable tool for discussing this very vague and yet real phenomena.

There is another murky area which is hard to measure and that is dizziness. I don't know about you, but when I get dizzy I get dizzy. What is there the doctor doesn't understand about being dizzy. Well they don't, and the reason is because there are lots of different manifestations of being dizzy. So just a word of advice. If you are having dizzy spells and you go to a doctor it will be helpful perhaps if you can describe the experience in word other than dizzy. For example, does the room spin around in your vision? Or does the room spin part way in one direction and then reverse and continue reversing? Is the dizziness one of blurred vision which blurs and then refocuses and back and forth? Do you feel like you are tipping over, like continually falling forward or even back wards?

I know when you are dizzy you just want it to stop and perhaps the last thing you want to do is try to figure out what you are experiencing. Dizzy is dizzy right? Now make it go away. Unbeknownst to us lay people the various manifestations of the dizzy experience can provide clues as to what might be the cause of the dizziness. There are a lot of options for the doctor to look at and your clues can help them possibly get to the solution faster.

Of course it may not, but information from the patient makes the job for the doctor who is pressured to see patients faster and faster easier and more effective.

We are truly in an environment where patient knowledge about their symptoms, their body, their experiences is crucial. You will get more value out of your doctor visit the more you can succinctly tell them what is going on. Please refer back to the chapter on Your Visit. I really can't stress the importance of your preparation prior to your doctor visit.

Continuing with Objects as Inconceivable Chih-i mentions specifically difficult and serious diseases as those for which one should most definitely seek the wisdom a wise person and the medical advise of a physician. The wise person in this case is your Buddhist teacher, or for a non-Buddhist reading this the advice of your spiritual provider. In ancient times these two roles frequently if not always were the same person, especially in Eastern societies and throughout tribal enclaves in the Americas, Africa, Middle East and early European societies. This action encompasses the other nine of these ten modes of contemplations.

We humans have adopted many delusions about the nature of reality following mistaken views and conceptions and so we drown in samsara. Because we place greater emphasis on material over spiritual, or spiritual over material we create imbalance and pursue objective while ignoring important considerations for a balanced life. The drive towards personal gain and comfort ceases the flow of compassion, the drive for accumulation of resources ceases the flow of good deeds.

If we are able to arouse deep compassion and desire to share bliss of the true nature of reality, non-duality, dependent origination, we can overcome mistaken views in self and others in this way a person who is experiencing illness can arouse the realm of bodhisattva through their illness. In this realm the bodhisattva contemplates the emptiness of disease which allows for the healing and elimination of dis-ease. While the dis-ease is overcome and healed the bodhisattva is able to arouse tentative illness.

Recall from the beginning of this book that tentative illness or disease are those that are taken on by the bodhisattva in order to teach other how to live in illness and through disease and dis-ease.

Arousing deep compassion for others even while suffering form illness leads to the cultivation of the mind of the emptiness of the non-substantiality of the dis-ease. The illness having not true independent nature ceases to exist as a substantive thing. It is still present but it is inconceivable. In this state then the illness is transformed into a teaching device for the bodhisattva to lead by his life. The illness is transformed into the realm of bodhisattva. As Chih-i says this becomes the way of the "bodhisattva [of the Tripitaka Teachings] who have disease and heals by 'analyzing the essence' [of things as empty]"[6]

Not everyone however, is able to achieve this contemplation of emptiness, and it is important to understand the consequences of the emptiness of disease. Those who dwell primarily in the realm of Sravaka being unaware of this emptiness follow the flow of ignorance being unable to make distinctions concerning dis-ease and so are unable to realize the Buddha Dharma and this limits their ability to hep sentient beings attain enlightenment. It is as if they are stuck in the intellectual analysis of the manifestation, experiences, whys and wherefore's, the size and shape of the illness and so forth. I compare it to the doctor who comes in takes your temperature, pulse, looks in your eyes, your throat, your ears even before saying hello or asking why you are in his office. Then when you begin to speak he cuts you off and starts telling you how you feel. Have you ever had a doctor do that to you? I have, its like you aren't even in the room. One time I told the doctor whenever you're finished telling me how I feel let me know when you are ready to hear from me how I feel, meanwhile I'll just hang

---

6   ibid, page 1357

out here and ignore you.

So the mind of facts, figures, analysis, data is not always the most conducive to being able to cultivate and understand the empty nature of dis-ease or even disease and illness. Also the factual oriented, logical, thinking only with little or no feeling is not generally oriented to compassion since compassion is vague and feeling oriented lacking data and statistics. The mechanical doctor is better suited to fixing robots than humans.

If however your care provider is capable of looking you in the eye, asking about you feelings as well as your symptoms then the diagnosis is generally going to head in a direction where treatment is more important than the statistics of medical journals. It is more likely you will be treated as a human and not a machine. It is more likely you won't experience the sensation of your doctor being bored to death not listening to you because you are too ordinary and just another humdrum sick person consuming oxygen in their office.

It is the same in Buddhism. When a person is unable to move beyond the technical details of doctrine and religious jargon then bridging the gap between lives is difficult if not impossible. When however we can share doctrine from the heart without relying on cliche or pat short cut phrases we can communicate as humans. Machines are more efficient with data sets, and short expressions that always mean the same thing. For humans no expression ever means the exact same thing to any two people and often it may vary according to the mood or mind state each person is in.

**Chih-i talks quite a lot about compassion and how important it is to cultivate when one has dis-ease, disease, and illness. As I have been studying this text I am struck by the direction he suggests compassion needs to flow.

Usually when compassion is mentioned, at lease in the medical settings I've been in and the other conversations I've read and heard outside hospitals, the direction of compassion goes from the healthy towards the sick. You don't normally hear much mention of the need for the sick to develop compassion. The general concept seems to be that the healthy, the wealthy, the well off, the capable people are urged to be compassionate for those less healthy, less fortunate, less capable. It is almost as if we don't expect the poor, the downtrodden, the challenged people to have a capacity for compassion and so we don't talk about it.

Yet evidence, at least circumstantial evidence or antidotal evidence shows that compassion exists in even the poor, ill, less fortunate, less well off. I myself grew up witnessing the black jazz musicians in New Orleans who had very little beyond their instruments and sometimes shared dwellings rally around others in their community supporting them even while having so little themselves.

Recently I finished reading Michelle Obama's book Becoming and in there she recounts her life as a child in Chicago where a challenged community would rally around and support those who were undergoing situations more severe than their own already severe situations.

Still even that goes from those relatively better to those relatively not as better. But what Chih-i says is that compassion from those in dis-ease and illness ought to develop the mind and actions of compassion even for those unaffected by illness. Even the healthy will become ill and the healthy are no immune to dis-ease. The compassion developed by the ill is a medicine for their cure. Their compassion in the midst of illness leads them out of dis-ease and enables them to cure others. This he says is the act of a bodhisattva who has illness and is able to cure others with the Perfect Teaching.

2. Arousing Compassion

Through compassion and arousing the mind of compassion it is the overcoming of dis-ease with a single thought and is the single overcoming through compassion.

The compassion Chih-i talks about he calls perfect and universal compassion and it is the manifestation of the universal teaching of the Buddha.

The thought that almost immediately comes to mind beyond the examples in the Vimalakirti Sutra is the actions of the Buddha with regard to Devedatta. For those reading this who are unaware of the story about Devedatta I will recount it briefly here.

Devedatta was the cousin of the Buddha who due to deep jealousy sought first to usurp the Buddha's portion in the Sangha, eventually leading to the first break up of the Sangha. After the Buddha head that division and the machinations of Devedatta were thwarted Devedatta tried on several occasions to kill the Buddha, each time failing.

So here is someone clearly suffering from dis-ease and what does the Buddha do? The Buddha with infinite patience and compassion never abandons Devedatta even after multiple attempts to destroy the Jewels of Buddha, Dharma, and Sangha. In Buddhism there is nothing more precious or more revered and protected than the Buddha, Dharma, and Sangha.

Devedatta tried to destroy the Jewel of Sangha by splitting it, he tried to destroy the Jewel of Dharma by perverting it with various rules that were in opposition to the teachings, he tried to destroy the Jewel of Buddha by his attempts to kill the Buddha. If ever there was a bad guy it was Devedatta, and to this day he is considered an evil person due to his actions. He is the perhaps universal name given when speaking of evil.

Yet, the Buddha never shunned him, the Buddha never ostracized him, he never kicked him out of the Sangha, though Devedatta certainly did separate himself from the Sangha. The Buddha never sought praise for his compassion, he gave it freely even though he was mistreated by the recipient of the compassion, he continued to extend compassion to Devedatta. In fact in the Lotus Sutra it is revealed the past relationship between Devedatta and the Buddha as well as the future enlightenment of even this most evil of persons.

In Nichiren Buddhism the name Devedatta even appears on our most important object of veneration which we devote our selves to single-mindedly. What I imagine true compassion is, and I say imagine because I can not say I have developed that depth of compassion yet, is the compassion that can see deep into the heart or soul of a person and see their innate Buddha life. That is hard to do. Yet it is that sort of compassion that lifts Devedatta out of eternal hell realm and raises him to enlightenment. Not as a charitable act to be praised for but as the core fundamental truth of the life of Devedatta and of all of us.

With that sort of compassion disease and illness crumble before us can enable us to become healers even in our own limited state of capacity. Whether our illness is disease or dis-ease we possess the power and capability to heal others because we have healed ourselves even though we may remain sick of physical body. The illness of body lacks essential substance with right contemplation and because there is no substance there is no true illness, dis-ease is shed and the power of the ability to cure others can reside within our very own life even when wracked with sickness.

My own experiences both of my own and those I've witnessed in others from the boys dying of AIDS to the many I've been with in the hospital have witnessed and experienced this truth. It is impossible for me to say that I have not been cured by those dying boys who I sat with who I attended in their last moments of premature death. My life was and has been profoundly changed, cured even of many dis-eases.

Watching a guy whose skin was literally melting off his body, whose every movement and touch would result in more skin being

128

ripped and even breathing caused excruciating pain please to receive Catholic communion so the could die a Catholic and be buried alongside his wife, can not hep but leave one affected by the spirit of the man to fulfill a promise to his wife so both he and her could be in peace even though he died hours later. Even his receiving the wafer and wine were acts full of pain. The young priest who came to the hospital when I call the dioceses who was on his first ever hospital visit to give the communion and perform the ritual of conversion was affected. He was trembling and kept putting his sacred objects on the bed and I had to keep picking them up and sanitizing them, he was moved by this act of devotion and compassion of the husband.

Like Dana, the giving of support for the Dharma with no expectation or reward true compassion is given regardless of benefit or reward and also given even if it will be refused or used in ways not intended.

I have as I am sure you have as well, heard comments about giving to homeless or street panhandlers or beggars, that giving just enables them to buy booze. That is not compassion. Compassion is not just giving when it is convenient or the outcome is controlled. It would be better and certainly more honest to just say you don't want to give rather than attach a moral value or statement to the selfishness of withholding aid. Give if you can, if you can't then walk on buy but don't try to elevate your life at the expense of those less fortunate. The Buddha didn't act with compassion to Devedatta with conditions.

Besides you don't know what your relationship to that other person is, perhaps in a previous life you were the beggar and your fortune in this life is the result of his previous compassion to you, and now you are begrudging your compassion. None of us arrived at any fortune we may have without the support of many people and many acts of caring, giving, teaching, and compassion.

A parent does not rest until their child is cured. When a child become ill so do the parents. This is the life of compassion of bodhisattvas. As long as sentient beings have illness, dis-ease then the bodhisattva has illness and with their great compassion cures all beings. When all beings are cured the bodhisattva is cured.

3. Skillful Means for a Peaceful Mind

Chih-i talks about becoming ill in the meditation chamber in this section . For us the meditation chamber is our practice realm, this realm. It originate from the Omandala of the Lotus Sutra which was inscribed by Nichiren for our benefit. However because of the principle of oneness of self and environment and subject and object everywhere we go becomes the Buddha Realm in this Saha world. This is determined and manifest from our mind, from our faith, and from our practice. Becoming ill, suffering from dis-ease or disease our first practice is to understand and embrace the essence of emptiness as outlined above. This is Chih-i's instruction.

He further guides us to arouse our aspiration for enlightenment. I recently had a discussion at our Sunday morning service about what enlightenment is. When I asked folks in the Sangha most had at best a vague notion of something they thought might be enlightenment. I find it interesting that this thing we talk about this goal we hold up for ourselves to attain most people have not idea of what it is. The resultant problem here is this means none will know if and when they begin to approach much less accomplish enlightenment.

I highly recommend that beginning now, even before and perhaps especially before you become ill, to form a picture of what you think enlightenment is. What is it that you are in quest of? What will your life be like in enlightenment? What could be some indications to you, some sign posts if you will, that you are close or beyond? A goal ill perceived is a goal likely to be missed.

Here is one point though, I believe that you will find that your expectation of what enlightenment might be like will expand and grow over time, and this is in itself a form of enlightenment. Every ah-ha moment is a small step to enlightenment. Enlightenment is not a fixed destination rather an evolving consciousness. However you may miss it as you journey though life. What ever your thoughts are about what enlightenment is, they are valuable and can help you in the achievement of that which we seek, and it most certainly is even more than your initial thoughts.

Enlightenment expands before you. It probably has already expanded before you, yet you were not aware of it even being. So first firmly anchor your core self, your true self, not your role, not your looks, not your attributes, not your skills, but deeper than all of those your true self. Firmly hold that and anchor it to the attainment of enlightenment. Enlightenment is not about your looks, your personality, your economic status, your eduction, your job, your age, none of those things are factors when it comes to your true self and your enlightenment. The Lotus Sutra clearly teaches that. Young boys who know nothing of Buddhism other than to offer a mud pie to this person coming through their village and whom everyone is making a fuss over become Buddhas themselves due to that simple act in innocence and ignorance.

Next is the instruction to straighten one's body. This can be problematic for many who are sick, especially with some internal injuries and with skeletal challenges. Here is my thinking on this, and I insert my thinking here because Chih-i doesn't talk about this in his writing, the challenges of not being able to straighten one's body.

Currently I am going to the Veterans Administration Hospital here in Syracuse three days a week for various exercise classes. My motivation for doing this is to regain some lost flexibility and to increase my range of motion in some joints as well as try to get some relief for my pain from the fractured vertebrae. In all the classes there are people with even worse skeletal and muscular challenges than I have. The teaching techniques are modified for the limitations we each face. In all cases the instructors stress that there is benefit to be gained simply by doing even a little bit of the exercise.

In particular the Yoga and Qigong instructors stress holding the image in your mind of the shape of your body as being completely able to do the exercise. In other words the image in your mind of your body doing the full exercise has the physiological affect of doing the exercise correctly. It isn't quite the same as doing the exercise but it is close with regard to mind-body.

When our mind visualizes the goal our body actually responds positively and enables the body to move closer to the objective. Whereas when our mind holds onto an image of the body limited the body complies with a limited affect. The mind has tremendous power over the body. This we have learned and discussed in other parts of this book.

So for those who are unable to attain a straight body, holding the image of your body as being erect and straight is a beneficial effort and serves the same purpose. It takes mental energy even in a body in good condition to hold the body erect. The same is true even for a body unable to remain or attain straightness.

So hold in your mind the image of your body erect even while it may be curled in bed. Your mind is the important thing in this case. If your condition should change continue to hold that image in your mind, even to the day when and if you can accomplish it with your body.

Some days you may not be able to do this at all and other days you might be able to go a long time. Do what you can and do it with joy. Also remember that one Odaimoku chanted with your mind silently with concentration and joy is powerful and can move mountains and sky. Think about the quality of your Odaimoku and let go of notions of quantity. It is better to chant one concentrated Odaimoku than hours of unfocused Odaimoku chanted out of a sense of obligation. I think of it sort of how I think about my life.

I am not looking for longevity that reduces my quality. Of course I am old enough to have enjoyed a quantity of life denied to many. So perhaps it is easier for me to say this than some. Don't go by my standards or my expectations for my life, hold clearly in your mind what your objective is and chant with joy in all cases.

Next, and I've covered this above, Chih-i instructs to focus your thoughts practicing only cessation, or only contemplation. These methods have been outlined in this writing so you may need to review them by the time you get to this point.

We need to remember that Chih-i wrote this long before the age of Degeneration which we live in. He wrote this before Nichiren revealed the single practice for this age of chanting the sacred title to the Lotus Sutra, the Odaimoku, Namu myoho renge kyo. His instructions to use good and skillful methods of instruction are incorporated in the single act of chanting Odaimoku. For those in Chih-i's time the practice was less concrete, more intellectual and complex. How fortunate for us that Nichiren gave us the practice of the Odaimoku. We should chant it with great joy, with concentration, with compassion, with an image of an erect and straight body. With this practice we are to regulate our mind, your practice to focus on these things as well as your goal of living in, through, and with your illness. Again remember that in Chih-i's time people usually either were cured or died and the idea of living long term with an illness, with disease was rare. For us we have been given both a blessing and sometimes perhaps a curse. It will be up to each of us to determine which is the case. The instructions given previously I believe offer some tools and aids in our contemplations on this matter.

Chih-i says that once you are seated in this way, and once you practice in this way you can experience "pure and cool awakening."[7] This state he says, and this I fully believe and have experienced, this is the "Great Medicine" so you do not need to confuse things with other healing methods (here do not take this to mean not seeking professional medical treatment, the two are not in

---

7   ibid, page 1360

opposition to each other remember).

4. Deconstructing Dharmas

In this section and in some previous sections I have used the
term dis-ease and in those cases I am speaking about mostly the
ramifications of illness that causes us to be not at ease in our
present condition. Because there is separate classification of
illness for mental illness and physical illness I use dis-ease to
speak about the upset in our mental state caused by illnesses of
either body or mind. Now technically mental illness is a physical
illness as the brain is a physical organ in the body. But in Western
medicine we have a distinction. Dis-ease is my attempt to speak
of something different than mental illness. Sometimes previously
I have used dis-ease and disease together meaning that both are
included, the physical ailment and the minds discomfort with
the illness. They are not quite interchangeable but sometimes a
solution is found or achieved in both. Since I am not in a two way
dialogue with you the reader I can only hope that this offers some
clarity. Perhaps my editors will suggest a better solution or perhaps
they will recommend including this in an earlier portion of the
book.

For the teaching on Deconstructing the Dharma I will need to use
dis-ease heavily as different from disease and that is why I felt I
needed to clarify this a little.

Here Chih-i relies upon the principal that the self is manifest
in the environment. There is a oneness relationship between
the condition of the self-mind or realm of one's self and the
environment in which it exists. If one is in the mind-hell-realm
then one perceives the environment in a hell fashion. And if one
is in the mind-Buddha-realm then the environment is the Buddha
land. Chih-i says that when we consider our illness if we view
it as a physical affliction then we should see mountains as ill,
rivers, as ill, and he even says corpses as ill. Since mountains,
rivers, and corpses do not become ill (ignoring the environmental

classification of environmentally ill) then there is no illness that is physical.

The mountains, forests, rivers, and so forth do not suffer from such afflictions and so deconstruct the illness as not a physical matter. This is perhaps going to be a huge challenge for many especially if one is so firmly attached to realness of the affliction. Chih-i accepts that this might be the case in which he advises to return to exercises of Contemplation at the beginning of the Cessation practices.

As I consider this it is sort of like in the beginning we realize that there is a tumor in my lung and the physical effect is limitations on breathing, there is the potential of it being cancer, and the uncertainty of what will evolve over time. Let's say this is the medical diagnosis of the situation. On the other hand the tumor is both real and not real, and it is also neither real nor not real. There is an in-between aspect that begins to transcend the real vs not real. The tumor exists physically according to medical science and yet it doesn't exist as a separate identifiable experience from my conceptual mind. It exists and it doesn't exist. And even in its non-existent conception it also continues to exist in its physical presence.

The Vimalakirti Sutra says that it is of the not of the element of earth, it is not apart from earth, it is not a matter of merging. So my tumor is an earth element or is of the earth as is my body. My tumor and my body are not the earth itself. My tumor and my body are not merged with the earth, they do not arise independently of earth, and they are still not earth. In this way the disease is not dis-ease, illness is not dis-ease and so it is not real. Again see the section on Objects as Conceivable and Inconceivable.

I will admit this is somewhat existential perhaps, or esoteric perhaps, definitely metaphysical in nature. This sort of thing may be strange to many in Nichiren Buddhism because in the normal course of teachings these types of explanations are rarely covered.

This doesn't mean they are not a part of Nichiren Buddhism.

Stepping back again. Let me try a different way or putting this. Perhaps you have a house guest who comes to visit you. It might be relative or a friend. The time comes for them to leave and they do not depart. Instead they continue to occupy the guest room you let them sleep in. Even after some heated argument and pleadings they continue to remain. Eventually it becomes clear they will not leave so you make them an offer, a truce if you will. The deal is that they can stay as long as they stay in the room, and you will feed them, on the promise they remain in the room and don't cause trouble. My tumor, any of my illnesses are all unwelcome house guests to some degree or another.

The more attention I give to them the more space the occupy in my house. They aren't going to leave any time soon, and perhaps they never will. I continue to feed them, sometimes I feed them good things that really will encourage them to leave, so good for me and not so good for them, but I haven't broken my agreement. Sometimes I might make them exercise even when they don't want to perhaps I make them clean up the room or do laundry, after all I never said I would do the wash. The exercise to them is unpleasant and maybe they will decide of their own accord that it isn't worth it and pack their bags and leave. One can only hope right?

So I try to live a life that is conducive to my good health and conversely it is not so good for the unwelcome house guest. But if I stand outside the door yelling at them to leave my life become preoccupied with the guest and my life turns into hell. If I treat the illness/house-guest as a Buddha would then I am doing things that are good for me and good for them to leave. My compassion is a good cause to entice them to leave me alone without me getting angry or suffering.

That's not quite right I suppose. But the more real we imagine our illness, the more substance we give it the more our whole environment becomes that illness. But it isn't possible for plates on the table to be ill, it isn't possible for the things in our lives to manifest this illness and yet the more real we perceive our illness the more our life turns inward to the illness the more our life manifests dis-ease, the more we see everything as the disease.

Returning to oneness of self and environment, this is a two way phenomena. If we experience a little of the Buddha realm in our environment then it impacts our mind-realm. In Chapter XVI of the Lotus Sutra the Buddha said we look around and we see this world in turmoil, in a great fire. Yet through faith in the Lotus Sutra we can put on the lens of the true nature of reality and see that the world is indeed quite peaceful and beautiful. We may consider our body wracked with pain and plagued with disease and that is an illusion. Our lives are indeed Buddha as the Buddha realm encompasses all the other nine realms and the nine realms contain Buddha. Our illness is both hell and Buddha, depending upon our mind. Our mind gains clarity through our faith and study of the Lotus Sutra. Our faith is nurtured and grows from our reciting the sutra and chanting Namu myoho renge kyo.

Stepping away a little from Chih-i I'm going to share with you a little insight I have gained only in the past two days.

I returned from a trip to Alabama to visit an important museum and memorial dedicated to the cruelty and injustice that has been inflicted on Africans and blacks in our country. I won't go into the details as that is material for a different writing.

As I have shared in this writing it has been discovered that I have a fractured vertebrae in my cervical column, as well as arthritis in other surrounding vertebrae. The pain symptoms began in November and continue. I am currently waiting to get an MRI through the VA which moves at an incredibly and frustratingly slow pace. The MRI was scheduled a month ago.

Recently the pain has increased and has moved into my head manifesting as pains and headache. The pain in my shoulder is increasing as well as sharp stabbing pains all down my arm. It is difficult to breath because the pain triggers in my chest muscles.

Over the past three days the pain has really intensified. Now some of it may be related to the pace of my travel schedule, and so I am hoping that with some rest it may subside some.

While on my trip, and especially during a meal with a long time friend while I was on layover in Charlotte, I noticed that it was difficult sometimes to remember things. Upon returning to the airport it dawned on me that the pain was interrupting my thinking process. I would have a thought or an idea and the pain would spike and it would distract my thoughts and then it was difficult to return to what I was thinking about.

I've worked with many patients who are in severe pain. In all of my experience I've never heard anyone speak about how pain interrupts thinking, holding onto a train of thought, remembering things, or such. In all the reading I've done on pain I've never read anything about it. That isn't to say nothing has been written, but that if I haven't heard or read about it then I am guessing that if others experience it they may not be aware or if they are they may not know to say it. It is curious and leaves me wondering how this impacts the ability of a patient to express their needs and the care provider to give appropriate relief.

When I experience severe pain I try to modulate my breathing and focus my mind on cessation of pain and it's affect in my body. That too pulls me away from previous thoughts, so the relief is also an interruption in thinking, maintaining an idea, remembering, and functioning. I'm going to try to be more attentive to this phenomena and my awareness of what goes on within the environment of my body while in pain.

5. Knowing What Penetrates and What Obstructs.

Using the tools of the Four Noble Truths, the Twelve-Link Chain of Causation, and the Six Perfections we are instructed to examine the methods of treatment, their affect, their efficacy, what they help and what is hindered.

To a certain extent the awareness I shard above about how pain interrupts and how the method of pain cessation also interrupts is perhaps a beginning to being able to look at the whole picture rather than isolated parts of the picture. Pain has an impact and the cessation of pain also has an impact. The cessation is important to maintain, and especially important to be aware of is how both interact and manifest within the context of total health.

The fact that the travel may have contributed to the increase in pain can not be ignored, to do so would be to abandon dependent origination. The awakening of realization of pain and thinking processes reminds me that there is suffering, there is pain, it has a cause and there are ways to mitigate or change the cause and to employ skillful ways to do so. Notice the Four Noble truth first acknowledge the effect we experience and then only focus on causes; there is a cause, there is a way to change the cause thereby affect a different experience, and there are tools to employ to make the change.

Beyond the initial admission of suffering, the affects of suffering, every thing else looks to causes to impact the experiences of our lives. On the one hand we look at our lives and then turn away from the potential to wallow in self pity and move towards making significant changes to begin to experience a new way of being based upon a new way of living.

In my situation there is pain, and I'll be honest I am sometimes suffering due to the pain. When I find that I am suffering I remind myself that it is a choice and the result of actions, even if only mental actions. When I can return to simply the pain I have found that I am better able to look at how to manage the pain, and most recently some of the impacts of that pain on my life. The new awareness has encouraged me to think about strategies for remembering differently perhaps using more reminder prompts, being more diligent about making notes, and being more attentive to not simply abandoning my thoughts the moment the pain arises, but to enter more gradually into the pain.

This process is still new, so you are being invited into an adventure along with me. I find this very exciting actually if truth be told.

The sixth item in the teaching on Cessation is very fascinating to me because it takes a real experience, pain, illness, disease, dis-ease and looks at it from thirty-seven steps, or angles and Chih-i specifically states that this can be done "while you are at your pillow [suffering from disease]. Understand that suffering is not suffering, and you will enter the pure and cool pond [of awakening].

It would be difficult or even impossible to write much here without plagiarizing or abusing quotes. Yet I know that to purchase the book it is contained in which costs close to $100 dollars is not an option for many people. Also I am aware that perhaps some who read this are not inclined to pursue this to the depth required to understand the book. I offer this as an apology to both the translator and to you the reader. I do hope that you can perhaps support the translator if not by purchasing this book then buy looking into other Buddhist texts Paul Swanson has translated, even some of Nichiren's writings.

This section say that we are to look at all the ways in which we construct dualistic thoughts about our illness. Consider such thoughts a the contrast between suffering and non-suffering, or suffering and pleasure. Include other notions such as thriving and decay, or pure or impure. When pondering these dualities we live in and cling to it is important to realize there is a different possibility. That Buddhism teaches us about a space, thin as it may be, that resides between the polarities. Also how it is possible to live in such a way that it is neither suffering, nor non-suffering, that the reality is beyond our conventional words of expression.

When we apply one of the dualistic ways of thinking to any situation we are automatically fixed or stuck in that dualistic experience and that our experiences then mirror that fixation. However when we can begin to master an understanding that in actuality reality consists of both and neither at the same moment of time.

Let me see if I can illustrate this. Suppose you make a cause that results in a specific effect. Let's say that you shoplift an item from a store. When I was very young I did such a thing. I was in a Woolworth's store back in the 50s and shoplifted a small bag of candy. The store did not catch me, my parents did however. My parents forced me quickly gobble all the candy in the bag and then drink hot water. All I can recall is that I vomited. Then after I cleaned myself up I had to go down to the store with my mother and in front of the manager I had to apologize and confess to my crime. My mother then paid for the candy and I had to do extra chores around the house.

As much as I often speak about the abuses of my parents, they were not evil people. In fact this one incident has stuck with me even though I am ashamed of having done it. I don't think I've shared this before.

So, I committed a crime. I received an effect from the cause I made. Yet it isn't over. What I think is important to remember or consider is that the pain of the effect from the cause I made can be looked at as either beneficial or harmful. What made it beneficial is what I did after that incident, I never stole again. I am the only one responsible for not stealing again, I am the one responsible for making that event beneficial to my life. The benefit or punishment is not inherent in the effect of eating, vomiting, apologizing, doing chores. It is my actions going forward that made the experience beneficial.

When we think about our situation and what we will do going forward it is important to remember that the outcome is not fixed.

The outcome is a potential that has no good, no bad, no duality and is truly neither good not bad. Does that make sense.

In our illness there is no fixed or only dualist way to live or experience or think. There is only unlimited potential. It is up to you as to whether you assign it or fix it in some dualistic fashion. The pain is neither good, nor bad, nor neither good/bad. It is an unfixed experience without value, it is a potential for you to live and how you do so whether you insist on living in a dualistic manner or whether you mind can embrace the unfixed unrealized potential.

Going back to my candy shoplifting, there was an equal potential that I could have experienced it as cruel, unjust to me, that the candy was too small and insignificant item to warrant the punishment. I could have harbored notions of being treated unjustly. I could have rationalized the event saying such things as the store could afford the loss, or that somehow I deserved the candy because I didn't have any. There are an infinite number of ways our minds are capable of constructing a reality.

It is possible that if I had gone down that pathway I might have begun a life of ever increasing episodes of behavior of theft or even worse. The punishment did not fix the outcome. The outcome remained as merely a collection of potentials waiting for me to act upon.

We are almost finished so hang on. You've done a wonderful job keeping up with all of this though I suspect it might be a bit overwhelming. I think that is an appropriate experience. Being overwhelmed is not always a bad thing or something to be avoided. At this point or perhaps sooner I suspect you may have even experienced a sense of loss, or confusion due to the complexity and quality of information. That too is good.

Sometimes if something is too simple it can be easily passed over and then quickly put aside as out attention wanders. Sometimes when something is complex though it can be off putting. Each individual will be different and reach their limit at different points. I will say that if your still hanging around reading this that you have done remarkably well. I would also say that at this point total comprehension or even complete recall is not the objective.

Being at peace with the mystery and depth of what Chih-i offers us is a part of the practice. I was going to say it can be like a slap in the face, well I just did didn't I. That image is perhaps tad overly graphic. However let this complexity serve as an invitation to continually reflect on the various parts of the teaching. Abandon the need to understand it all. Be at peace with partial, incremental understandings and insights. Perhaps after you get a sense of the total expanse of the teachings something will stick up in your mind. Use that as a direction marker for where to go for deeper understanding. Look at the entire big picture then step closer and examine smaller parts until gradually you can step back and understand the whole picture, the landscape, and the environment represented.

Seven in the teaching on Cessation is Auxiliary Methods. This is a very short section which encourages the use of what we now refer to as integrative medicine. In the hospital where I worked we offered aroma therapy. Every nurses station had an aroma therapy kit. We would take a cotton ball, an easy to locate item in a hospital, and put a drop or two of various aromatic oils. The oils we used were different depending upon the effect desired. Most commonly though we would use lavender for its calming influence. We would then put the cotton ball into a zip-lock bag and give it to the patient. The reason for the bag is to protect the patient. Essential oils are very strong and can cause skin damage. For someone who has diminished sense of touch or feeling the oil could burn the skin and the patient may not feel it. Also different patients have various limits to their personal comfort regarding odors. So a person who only likes subtle aromas can seal off the bag and control how much aroma they smell.

In addition to aroma therapy we also offered music therapy, massage therapy, acupressure, and Healing Touch an energy healing modality. In all cases these auxiliary methods were not to replace the medical treatments prescribed by physicians rather to enhance them. When a patient has reached their limit dose for pain medication it is often the case that their pain is not lessened. There is not more medication that can be prescribed and so other avenues can be explored.

In my own provision of Healing Touch to patients in great pain and with no medicinal option available I witnessed countless times when the pain experience lessened and the patient went to sleep peacefully to get some much needed healing rest. I've provided Healing Touch to cancer patients who have told me afterwards that it allowed them to enter into and experience a sense of freedom and release from the pain and the fear. I seen patients who, keeping a lavender cotton ball handy and been able to reduce their anxiety.

When I was at the hospital we had a wonderful music therapist who played guitar and would go to different rooms and play favorite songs. Not only did it benefit the patient, many patients in adjoining rooms were cheered up, and the nurses were doubly uplifted because the music moved them and eased their burden with troubled, anxious, fearful, patients and patients in pain. Music can truly move the soul, mend the heart, and cure the body.

What is your favorite song. Our music therapists would frequent comment that many people when asked what their favorite song is simply can not recall it on the spot. So, why not take a pause from your reading and name your favorite song, so that way if you ever need to tell someone it may come to your mind much easier. Mine is the Beatles song "Here Comes the Sun" and a close second is the Moody Blues "Knights in White Satin". Now it's your turn.

Number eight in Cessation is Graded Stages of Attainment and here is another one which Chih-i specifically mentions being in bed or at your pillow. He urges the patient suffering from disease and illness to contemplate on your dis-ease, and your illness. By doing this gradually the true principle of the cause and result of your dis-ease. He compares to the beautiful lapis lazuli which is deep under the water. You can see it, this is your perception, this is like an abstract appreciation and much the same as your initial awareness of your illness. You can see it, you can name your illness, and you may have a theoretical understanding of the progression and possible cure. Since you may not have begun to experience the full affect of the named disease in your body it is still somewhat of an abstraction.

Perhaps you have fully experienced the symptoms of the disease, or perhaps your experience is in the initial stages of the progression of the illness. Still there is no full understanding of how you will continue to experience your illness. Also the text book explanation may not be appropriate in your unique circumstance. There may be other factors in your body that the medical texts do not consider. Sometimes various illness do occur simultaneously in most people, but still there may be other extenuating circumstances that may make your experience a little different or significantly different. Also as the illness progresses either to cure or continuation, it may progressively and more deeply interact with or conditions in your body and care.

The medical text is like the view of the lapis lazuli deep underwater which you can only see through the ripples and diminished light thereby distorting your perception of the precious stone. So perhaps you have previously seen lapis lazuli and you have an idea of what it looks like and that helps you 'see' the lapis under the water, your previous knowledge is an aid yet it isn't exactly like the lapis in the water. This stage of contemplation is called abstract, and further this refers to 'name and word' only.

This initial stage is not the stage at which illness is not removed, and even dis-ease is not removed, suffering is not removed. This stage is not our ultimate goal, and to become discourage or even stop means that your contemplation will progress no further towards elimination dis-ease and suffering.

The next stage in this Graded Attainment is 'approximate understanding'. At this point you can experience a lightening of the affects of dis-ease and suffering. Here you begin to more deeply embrace and understand the causes of your illness or your dis-ease. Also at this stage your aspiration towards the path, your motivation for continuing your practice and your faith grows stronger. Deepening understanding of the nature and cause of illness and dis-ease go hand-in-hand with increased aspiration for faith and practice. Please understand that pain may still be present and depending upon your particular illness a cure may not be present or has not progressed fully toward cure.

At this stage and further stages you are able to practice greater forbearance and increased ability to practice the cessation such as skillful means for a peaceful mind as above, and insight into the true nature of the reality of dis-ease and suffering. With continued practice and contemplation gradually you will experience less and less suffering even though a cure has not take place. Also it is important to realize even doing this Chih-i says misfortune may still arise, and so do not become discouraged.

Chih-i states that continuing to pursue this path and practice you will be able to eliminate the causes of dis-ease and remove suffering. There is a caution, and it makes sense and should be kept in mind continually. Never think that you have attained a grade or some level that you in fact have not achieved. This opens the door to arrogance, slackening of practice, reduced diligence, and setbacks from a weak mind. Never should we think that our practice is superior.

Resting in Patient Forbearance is the ninth of these modes of contemplation in Cessation practice. This is to practice diligently chanting the Odaimoku whether voiced or in you head, continue to study and practice the ten modes outlined here, be diligent about ones mind and body, and do not be discouraged or let external hindrances and conditions obstruct your practice. Do not rest or stop your practice, if you do so you the temptation to completely abandon your practice will become greater and in fact dis-ease may increase. Calm your mind even in the midst of your illness and dis-ease, never retreat, nor be moved from your practice and continue to discern your actions.

Number ten of the ten modes, our last one is No Passionate Attachment to Dharma. Do not let the individual meaning of these words confuse you into thinking that it is wrong to enjoy and find peace in your practice. Here the danger is when there is lessening of the dis-ease or suffering and your mind becomes increasingly clear and pure be cautious and not covet these gains, this is attachment and will defile your energy and your practice. Do not cling to your success as having attained some greatness, this causes imbalance. Be grateful for your progress and for the benefit of your practice, do not brag or gloat. To do so will cause imbalance and replace the pure Dharma with your impure thoughts thus polluting your life. Your success is due to not only your practice but your practice of the True Dharma, Namu Myoho Renge Kyo.

We've covered a large landscape of healing and practice. It would be unrealistic to think that one reading would be enough to retain, understand, or even incorporate these practices into one's life. Please return to this over and over as you continue through your healing process either from disease or from dis-ease.

Chih-i wraps up his teaching on the whole section of Contemplating Disease with the reminder and encouragement to cultivate contemplation of the Great Vehicle, to continue your practice of reciting the sutra, chanting the sacred title, Namu Myoho Renge Kyo, study and practice with these guidelines, never give up, or slacken, be always diligent in "attaining the One Great Cart."

This concludes my presentation of Chih-i's teaching and of my experiences as a chaplain, as a care provider, and a Buddhist. Thank you for reading, I hope you find healing and great joy.

With Gassho,
Namu Myoho Renge Kyo

Kansho Shonin
Ryusho Jeffus, MDiv, BCC

14

Afterword

During the time I wrote this book several monumental events have taken place in my life. In early April my dog, my companion of over 10 years died early one morning. Here it is May, a little over a month since then. I think at first I was more in shock or numb from the tragedy. More and more though I look for her around the house. When I get up in the morning I want to call to her and tell her it's time to go eat. Or when I come home I am compelled to call out and say I am home. The hole in my life is great, and I miss her. I am as yet undecided if I will get another dog. If I were younger I certainly would, being older though there are some things I need to consider before I take on the responsibility for a new companion pet.

The second event was being diagnosed with an eye condition which if untreated would eventually lead to blindness. The cure for the condition is to have cornea transplants. In mid April I had the first transplant done in my right eye. In July I will have the left eye transplant done.

As a chaplain I engaged in countless conversation with patients and patient families about organ and tissue donations. It is for many a difficult choice to make based upon many factors some religious and some personal. For others the decision is easy and most agree to become donors.

Sometimes people are reluctant to donate because they feel they are too old and nothing would be of any use to anyone. This is so far from the reality today in medical science with regard to organ and tissue donations. Age is not a factor especially for corneas, skin, and bone marrow or even bone material. It is beyond the scope of this book and this space to go into the details of all the uses for those items.

For me, now living with donated tissue it is a mystical, and humbling experience. I often find myself simply saying to the universe "thank you to whomever donated this cornea". To think someone died and upon their death the tissue was removed and then given to me. That person continues to live on though they are no longer living in this world a part of them lives in my eye and enables me to continue to see. I am grateful for the gift.

In closing I hope you have gained some benefit from reading and considering what I have offered and my understanding of the teachings provided by Chih-i and the application of that wisdom to our modern lives.

Connect with Ryusho Jeffus on-line:

Twitter:
@ryusho @myoshoji

Facebook:
https://www.facebook.com/Ryusho

Facebook Author Page:
https://www.facebook.com/revryusho

Blog:
https://www:ryusho.org/blog

Amazon Author Page
https://tinyurl.com/y6z9rcbm

Made in the USA
Middletown, DE
26 May 2021